A NATION OF
WUSSES

A NATION OF
WUSSES

How America's Leaders Lost
the Guts to Make Us Great

ED RENDELL

WILEY

John Wiley & Sons, Inc.

Published by John Wiley & Sons, Inc., Hoboken, New Jersey
Published simultaneously in Canada

For general information about our other products and services, please contact our Customer Care Department within the United States at (800) 762-2974, outside the United States at (317) 572-3993 or fax (317) 572-4002.

Wiley also publishes its books in a variety of electronic formats and by print-on-demand. Some content that appears in standard print versions of this book may not be available in other formats. For more information about Wiley products, visit us at www.wiley.com.

Library of Congress Cataloging-in-Publication Data:

Rendell, Edward G. (Edward Gene), date
  A nation of wusses : how America's leaders lost the guts to make us great / by Ed Rendell.—1
    p. cm.
  Includes bibliographical references and index.
  ISBN 978-1-118-27905-2 (hardback); ISBN 978-1-118-33066-1 (ebk);
  ISBN 978-1-118-33350-1 (ebk); ISBN 978-1-118-33461-4 (ebk)
    1. United States—Politics and government—2009- 2. Political culture—United States. 3. Self-sacrifice—Political aspects—United States. I. Title.
E907.R46 2012
973.932—dc23

2011053471

Printed in the United States of America
10 9 8 7 6 5 4 3 2 1

To Midge and Jesse Rendell,
without whose patience, forbearance, and support
none of the things I have achieved would have been possible.

It is not the critic who counts; not the man who points out how the strong man stumbles, or where the doer of deeds could have done them better. The credit belongs to the man who is actually in the arena, whose face is marred by dust and sweat and blood; who strives valiantly; who errs, who comes short again and again, because there is no effort without error and shortcoming; but who does actually strive to do the deeds; who knows great enthusiasms, the great devotions; who spends himself in a worthy cause; who at the best knows in the end the triumph of high achievement, and who at the worst, if he fails, at least fails while daring greatly, so that his place never be with those cold and timid souls who neither know victory nor defeat.

—*Theodore Roosevelt, speech at the Sorbonne,*
Paris, France, April 23, 1910

CONTENTS

Introduction

Thirty-three years in politics. Twenty-four in elected office. Fifteen months as chairman of the National Democratic Party. When I look back on these years I am amazed, filled with wonder, and most of all, filled with gratitude for the incredible opportunities I have been given.

But I came by it honestly. It came from Jesse T. Rendell, my father.

My dad was the finest person I have ever known. He died when I was fourteen and I thought my world had ended. People still tell me how unlucky I was to have lost my dad at fourteen, and I tell them that, in retrospect, I consider myself lucky that I had fourteen years of his guidance, tutelage, and love.

He taught me so much, first and foremost, by the way he lived. He truly believed in the Golden Rule, and he lived it every day. He was smart, aggressive, and hard-driven, but he *always* treated everyone with respect and dignity. At his funeral, I was a wreck, but I will always remember that all six of his employees attended. They were African American and Hispanic men who worked with him in the garment district in New York City. They acted as middlemen, taking orders from manufacturers, processing the fabrics, getting them dyed to order, and making sure they were delivered in time to meet the manufacturers' production deadlines.

My father was the business, and when he died, it immediately closed for good. But those six employees still came to his funeral out of respect. No person could have a better testimonial to him than that. And these lessons that Dad taught me have never left. I think about them and him almost every day. What would he do about a difficult decision I was confronted with? As DA, mayor, or governor, I've often had to talk to the children of policemen and firemen who lost their dads, and I tell them my experience — that their dads will never really leave them, that they will think of them every day of their lives.

How did this converter in the textile industry inspire his son to pursue a career in politics? He never served a day in office, was never even a committeeman, but he loved the Democratic Party. Of all my accomplishments—getting elected DA, mayor, governor— the one that would have filled him with wonder would have been having his son become chairman of his beloved Democratic Party. He thought it was the last hope for the little guy, the working stiff, the disabled, the poor, the very young, and the very old. He idolized FDR and loved Adlai Stevenson. Dad imbued me with the same love and passion. When I was only eight years old, he and I tacked up "Stevenson for President" signs, and the only time I ever saw this proud, strong man cry was the night in 1952 when Stevenson lost to Eisenhower. There were no polls back then, and minimal TV coverage compared to today. We were at a grocery store at about 9:45 p.m. and the radio blared that Ike had carried enough states to clinch victory. As we walked the two blocks home, I saw for the first and last time tears streaming down his face. Yes, I came by it honestly.

I believe that my dad would be very proud of how I have governed and the things I have done (at least most of them!), because in each office I've held I have tried to follow the ideals he taught me. Government can and should be a force to improve the quality of people's lives, to help create opportunity for those who have none, to help protect the most vulnerable among us who cannot protect themselves, to make sure that even the poorest and most downtrodden in our society have the basic necessities to survive. They call us public servants because our job is to serve the public. That seems a simple enough set of core beliefs, one that embodies what America is supposed to be.

But that very simple and decent view of our country is severely challenged today by those who view government as the enemy, who believe it cannot do anything effectively, and therefore the less government we have the better. Their message is simple and easy to understand: every dollar the government spends is a dollar out of your pocket. Especially in these challenging economic times, it taps into the anger and disillusionment that so many of our citizens feel. But it is simply wrong. It's also self-serving: don't expect me do to anything as a politician because politicians can't do anything right. It charts out a course I strongly believe will have disastrous consequences for our country. We'll stop being the USA and start being the CYA. There isn't a single successful business in America that hasn't invested in its own growth, and if we stop doing it, our beloved nation will lose its competiveness and we will risk becoming a second-rate economic power.

If we cease our 236-year commitment to care for all our people we will become a bitter and divided country, filled with rancor and hate. But most of all, if we stop doing bold things, if we stop creating new ideas that can impact the entire world, if we cease to have a vision of how we want to make things better, if we circle the wagons and seek to just protect what we have, then we will lose the spirit that has made America the greatest country in the world—the American spirit that has overcome every obstacle put in our path, the American spirit that has never seen a challenge or a problem it couldn't handle, the American spirit that has kept the world free and invented so many ideas that changed the world, the American spirit that has stood out like a beacon, attracting millions to our shores from every corner of the world.

We are in real danger of losing that spirit, that boldness, that courage. I fear that in so many ways, we are becoming a nation of wusses. A nation so afraid to take risks, to face challenges, to do great things. America was born as the idea of great patriots who were the original risk-takers. Think of it, a collection of shopkeepers and farmers believing that on their quest to be free they could defeat the British army and navy—the greatest fighting force in the world. And they knew the risk they were undertaking. As Benjamin Franklin said, "We must all hang together or surely we will all hang separately."

Would Americans in 2012 undertake a similar risk for such a worthy goal? I hope so, but I'm not sure. I'm sure you can think of more than a few leaders, local and national, private or public, who would say, "Why rock the boat?" We seem to be unwilling to take on anything risky or complicated. We just can't lose the spirit that made us great. The battle for the soul, the heart, and the direction of America is one we must win. I intend to do everything I can to ensure that that happens. I hope this book serves as a wake-up call.

Of course, politics isn't all soaring rhetoric. That's the challenge. It's noble, but it's also dirty. It's frustrating, but it's also funny. I have always had the ability to laugh at things (including myself). It's the only way I have survived, and even thrived, for thirty-three years in politics. But even the numerous stories I recount here make a point about things we need to change to make politics and our system of government work better. In the end, big government or small government isn't the answer. It's effective government. And you can't be effective if you're a wuss.

Well, here goes!

CHAPTER 1

The Wussification of America

I n my thirty-three years in public life I believe I have done many cutting-edge things, taken real risks to make change happen, and I surely have said things that have created great controversy (a few of which I'd like to have back). But incredibly, nothing I have done or said gained as much worldwide attention, created as much controversy, as what I said about a football game.

As many people know, I am great fan of the Philadelphia Eagles football team. In fact, when I was mayor, Comcast SportsNet asked me if I wanted to be part of a TV show after each Eagles game. I said sure. I went to every Eagles home game and watched every away game faithfully, so I thought it might be fun. And it sure was. I was on a panel with a former Eagles player, the charismatic Vaughn Hebron; a great sportswriter, Ray Didinger; and the host, one of the best sportscasters in America, Michael

Barkann. Thirty minutes into my first show, I thought, "We're actually getting paid for this? A bunch of guys sitting around talking about a football game?" Well, the show was a hit, and twelve years later it has become so popular that we now do a pregame show as well.

On December 26, 2010, the Eagles were scheduled to play an important game against the Minnesota Vikings. If the Eagles won, it could help them secure a bye in the playoffs. But unbelievably, the game was canceled Sunday morning before one drop of snow had fallen, based on forecasts of a significant storm. One hour before game time the city had less than six inches on the ground. The western suburbs had less than three inches, and Wilmington, to our south, less than two inches. Good grief! Canceling a game because of that amount of snow—unthinkable! Vince Lombardi must have been rolling over in his grave. Americans in Montana, Wyoming, and South Dakota—heck, even fans in Chicago, Boston, and Pittsburgh—must have been astounded!

At about five o'clock that afternoon our Comcast show producer, Rob Kuestner, called me at home and asked if I would do a phone interview about the cancellation. I said sure, and when he asked me what I thought of the NFL and the Eagles' decision to cancel the game, I blurted it out that we were becoming "a nation of wusses" and that this was just further evidence of the "wussification of America."

I never thought these comments would set off controversy that would gain the attention it did. The *Washington Times* asked me to write an op-ed piece about the "wussification," and they put it, unbelievably, on the front page. I wrote:

> It was December 14, 1958, I was a 13 year old boy living in New York City. I was at Yankee stadium watching my (then) beloved Giants play the Cleveland Browns. We had to win to force the Browns into a playoff to decide who would be in the NFL Championship game. There were less than two minutes to go, it was dark and worse yet there were swirling

winds and a driving snowstorm. Pat Summerall, the Giants placekicker, lined up 49 yards away. If he didn't make it they would be eliminated. Given the conditions, I didn't believe he had a chance. He was a straight away kicker and he drove it with everything he had.

Today, some 52 years later, I can still close my eyes and see the ball soaring through the darkness, through the snow and through the wind. He made it! He made it! The Giants won!

That game remains indelibly etched in my memory because it captures the magic of football—a game that is played regardless of the weather conditions. The NFL robbed me and thousands of other fans of the chance to have some new magical memories by cancelling the Eagles-Vikings game which was to be played in Philadelphia Sunday night. It was inconceivable that they would call off a football game. In the movie "A League of Their Own," Tom Hanks, the manager of a women's professional baseball team uttered the famous lines, "Crying? There's no crying in baseball!!" Cancel a football game because of bad weather? There's no cancelling a game for bad weather in football!! This is the sport where Adam Vinatieri kicked a winning field goal through the driving snow in the famous "Tuck" game. Where the Bengals and the Chargers played an AFC championship game in a minus 64 degree wind chill factor. Where Bart Starr dove into the end zone to win the NFL championship against the Cowboys in near zero temperatures.

The NFL explained that the forecast called for perhaps a foot or more of snow and they didn't want thousands of fans to be "trapped" after the game in stadium parking lots. Conditions never got close to that dire prediction. Major expressways remained open, and there were no significant accidents throughout the night. The city's subway system, one of the best in the nation, functioned perfectly. Philadelphia's center city, a ten-minute subway ride to the stadium, had thousands of available parking spots on a Sunday night.

Yet the NFL thought it had to protect the fans. What's wrong with that, you might ask? Simple. First, to call off this game because of snow is further evidence of the "wussification" of America. In 1948 the Eagles won the NFL Championship playing at home through a blizzard that put nearly a foot of snow on the field. We seem to have lost our boldness, our courage, our sense of adventure, that frontier spirit that made this country the greatest nation in the world. A little snow, a potential traffic tie-up, a long trip home caused us to cancel a football game? Will Bunch, a writer for the *Philadelphia Daily News*, said that if football were played in China, sixty thousand Chinese would have walked through the snow to the stadium, doing advanced calculus as they did so. He's probably right, and it's no secret why the Chinese are dominating the world stage.

Second, the NFL didn't trust the fans to use their own judgment about whether going to the game in the snow was worth the risk they might encounter. If I had planned to take a seven-year-old with me to the game, I probably would have decided to stay home and watch it on TV, but if I were going with some of my friends I would have driven to center city, parked, and taken the subway to and from the stadium. But that's *my* decision to make, not the NFL's. We all hear talk about the "nanny" state, but now we have the "nanny" NFL, so concerned about the welfare of the fans, and perhaps potential liability, that it feels it has to protect us from ourselves.

In fact, it was all about potential liability. I have nothing against making a decision that will keep people safe, but I'm not talking about that. I'm talking about leaders making a decision based on the sole calculation that it will keep their job safe. Today it seems like everywhere you look you find an army of lawyers advising us against doing things and a flotilla of worrywarts right behind, cheering them on, telling us we can't take that risk—and not because they're really worried about us. This seems to have produced ludicrous results. Schools close in eastern cities when there are two inches of snow on the ground; sometimes they close before a flake has fallen. Think of all the school boards, corporate boards, and editorial boards that keep throwing money on dumb projects, sticking to the same talking points, because no one has the guts to say, "Let's do something else instead." The first law of organizations is that a bureaucracy in motion tends to stay in motion until someone willing to take the heat stops it. Compounding that is the fact that it is always easy to do nothing than to do something. So you cancel school, or you cancel the game, or you don't build that factory, or you don't announce a new plan to fix things. All of these absurdities are products of anti-risk-takers who seem to have come to dominate American life. If these things were all this attitude produces, it would be annoying, nothing more. After all, what sparked my comment was just a football game.

But what is so desperately important is that our newfound "wussiness" is affecting big things that really do matter to our country and to our people.

The American infrastructure is literally beginning to fall apart, and our leaders understand this but are unwilling to invest in fixing it. They're afraid it's too hard, too complicated. They don't want to risk spending the money that's necessary because they're afraid of losing the next election. Can you imagine what would have happened if our leaders of yore felt the same way? There would be no Erie Canal, no intercontinental railroad, no national highway system, no Hoover Dam. All of these projects were hard and difficult to get done. All of them involved significant expenditures of taxpayer money. But we did them because they were important, they were necessary for our growth, they were worth the risks. Of course, there were wusses and naysayers back then, but we didn't put them in charge of things. As John F. Kennedy said about his plan to put a man on the moon by the end of the sixties, "We choose to go to the moon in this decade and do the other things, not because they are easy, but because they are hard."

When I quoted Will Bunch about how the Chinese would have handled a game in a snowstorm, I was quoted in Shanghai and Beijing newspapers. I am certain they believe that we have, in fact, become wusses and that that belief informs the way they deal with us. As my friend Donald Trump points out, the Chinese are pushing us around without fear of reprisal. They subsidize Chinese-made products and sell them here at such low prices that it drives American manufacturing out of business. They dumped pipe into the United States at such low prices that it literally ended the production of pipe by the steel industry, costing Pennsylvania three thousand good jobs. Steel company executives, the steelworkers' union, and elected officials complained and took the case to the International Trade Commission. It took several years to succeed, and by the time the case was won and a quota was put in place, thousands of jobs had already been destroyed. However, the dumping was stopped, and thousands of jobs were saved going forward.

The Chinese steal our intellectual property, manipulate their currency to give themselves huge economic benefits over us, and send us crappy products—and not just cheaply made jeans. I'm talking about lead-laced toys and poisoned dog food and who knows what else. They seem secure in the belief that we won't fight back because we are scared because they hold so much of our debt. Why don't we fight back? Why don't we get tough with them? They are probably waiting for us to do so. Can you imagine what impact it would have if we even threatened to limit the amount of Chinese goods that could come into the United States? Their economy simply couldn't stand it, and my guess is that though they wouldn't like it, they would respect us a whole lot more than they do now.

Do you think Teddy Roosevelt or Harry Truman wouldn't have fought back?

If we are to continue to lead the world economically and in other ways, we must regain that American spirit, that boldness and courage, that willingness to take on challenges no matter how hard or how great the risk if the reward makes that risk worth taking. We need leaders with the courage to risk the thing that matters most to them: their own jobs!

No wusses need apply.

CHAPTER 2

"We're Mad as Hell and We're Not Going to Take It Anymore!"

I t was election night, November 1969, in Philadelphia and my boss, District Attorney Arlen Specter, was running for reelection. I had worked for him as an assistant district attorney for two years of his first term.

Arlen was a tough, sometimes mean, and always demanding boss. But he was smart as a whip and made us believe that our office of sixty-five attorneys and fewer than two hundred people were the sole guardians who kept Philadelphia from falling through the gates of hell. So his reelection campaign was my reelection campaign. I believed my name was on the ballot, too, and that the voters were going to make a judgment on how good a job we had done.

We all gathered at his election headquarters in a downtown hotel, under the banner that had the campaign slogan for

Arlen and his controller running mate, former basketball star Tom Gola, "They're younger, they're tougher, and nobody owns them." As the returns rolled in it became apparent that they were headed for an incredible landslide victory. Incredible because Philadelphia had become an overwhelmingly Democratic city and they were Republicans. In fact, their two election victories were the only Republican triumphs in the previous thirty-five years of Philadelphia elections.

I was elated. The voters of the city had affirmed that I had done a great job. In fact, I was so elated that I drank and drank and drank. And after that night, I almost never drank alcoholic beverages again—even to this day. Sure, I drank beer in college trying to look cool (something I have never managed to do in my sixty-eight years on this planet), but I had given it up. Not that night, however, not yet. That very special night when the people of Philadelphia gave my work a resounding stamp of approval.

In fact, I drank so much that when I returned to my third-floor bachelor apartment at 2:00 A.M., I ran up the stairs shouting at the top of my lungs, "We're younger, we're tougher, and nobody owns us!" Needless to say, I woke up the entire building and just managed to unlock my door in time to run to the bathroom and throw up six hours of eating and drinking. *Sic transit gloria!*

These two years began my thirty-three-year association with Arlen Specter. I know he is a controversial figure, often maligned, sometimes fairly, but he also is a good man and an even better public servant. He is fiercely loyal and immensely proud of the people who worked for him (an incredible group that, in addition to myself, includes many others who became elected officials, judges, and federal prosecutors). I have never seen anyone work harder, more effectively, and more tirelessly to protect the interests of his constituents. His career, much like mine, has had more than a few bumps in the road, but he never quit and he never will.

For most of his political life, Arlen was a Republican, and often the radical right-wingers of his party called him and others like him RINOs—Republicans In Name Only. The so-called

RINOs often are risk-takers, antitheses of the wusses who dominate American politics today. They are risk-takers because they are bucking their party because they believe it's the right thing to do. By doing so they are knowingly angering the right-wing purists and potentially creating an opponent for themselves in a Republican primary. It's happened to solid but independent-minded conservative Republicans such as Specter, Bob Bennett, John McCain, Richard Lugar, and Orin Hatch. Specter and Bennett lost their seats as a result; McCain survived and Lugar and Hatch will be challenged in 2012.

Voting your conscience is a good deed, but in today's political world no good deed goes unpunished, and as a result, wusses are sadly the rule, not the exception.

The first bump occurred when an overconfident Specter ran for a third term as DA, when he really wasn't interested in the job anymore and was preparing to run for governor. He was defeated by Emmett Fitzpatrick in a stunning upset. The night of that election, unlike four years earlier, was devastating. We all thought it was the end of the world. But in truth, it was the event that spurred my thirty-three-year career in politics and elective office.

After the election, all of the assistant district attorneys were interviewed by Mr. Fitzpatrick, the DA-elect. I had risen to the position of chief of the Homicide Unit, and it was clear during my interview that he wanted to change the hard-line approach the unit had taken, and he asked me if I could do that. I said no. Murderers deserved the appropriate punishment, and we shouldn't plea-bargain for lower sentences just to move the backlog. I knew, as I said it, that I had ended my chance of remaining as chief of the Homicide Unit. So I decided to leave the office.

I opened up my own practice, and I was determined not to take any criminal cases. I couldn't see myself as a defense lawyer, but I didn't have any civil experience, so I was basically spinning my wheels. I had read where Sol Linowitz had made a fortune by incorporating a business for two young men who had no money. Instead of a fee, he took a 20 percent interest in the corporation's future profits. The corporation turned out to be called Xerox. On six different occasions during my brief stint in private practice I tried to emulate Sol's success. Needless to say, I am the proud owner of 20 percent of six companies that never made a dime.

One day after about two years of drifting, I got a call from Pennsylvania governor Milton Shapp. He asked me to serve as deputy special prosecutor to investigate political and police corruption in Philadelphia; the special prosecutor was Bernie Segal, a great prosecutor from Erie. We worked hard for the next six months, but the Pennsylvania legislature, many members of which we were investigating, cut off our funds. We worked for more than two months, without pay, and at the end there were only six of us and a brilliant Harvard Law School intern, Ralph Jacobs, who was our typist. Eventually the office folded.

I was angry at how we had been treated by the political system at that time. The governor had to create a special prosecutor's office because the DA's office under Emmett Fitzpatrick had become part of the Democratic machine under the leadership of Philadelphia mayor Frank Rizzo. He refused to investigate any municipal corruption, of which there was plenty, and politics reached into the DA's office. Many connected people were protected from investigation or even prosecution. Even worse, in the public's mind was the fact that, as I sensed when I was interviewed, he had turned the office into a plea-bargain mill, where many dangerous murderers and felons received outrageously light sentences. And even worse than that, Fitzpatrick was arrogant and never understood or cared about the essence of public service. He had almost an open disdain for the public.

As a result of all this, he became a target of all the major newspapers, with one story after another. The crowning blow came when he attended a National District Attorneys Association Conference in Montreal. Upon his return, he put in a voucher for $184 for dinner, which he said he paid for several other cities' DAs at a seafood restaurant called Aquascutom. The *Philadelphia Inquirer*, one of our major dailies, discovered that Aquascutom was not a restaurant but a clothing store and the $184 was for a safari suit purchased by Fitzpatrick. The voucher was an attempt to get the public to pay for it!

The safari suit was the last straw. People were outraged, and it became the rallying symbol of a "dump Fitzpatrick" movement. As his reelection year rolled around, I kept waiting for some big-name Democratic lawyer or judge to challenge him in the primary. None did, primarily because they were afraid of the mayor and the Democratic machine. The mayor could be and often was vengeful, and the machine was still incredibly strong. It had carried the city for Jimmy Carter just two months earlier by more than 250,000 votes.

When it became apparent that no Democrat was coming forward to challenge Fitzpatrick, I decided to try. I didn't really believe I had a chance, but I was so angry about how he had destroyed the office I loved and so fed up with the way the machine had strong-armed the special prosecutor's office out of existence that I wanted to make trouble for them.

Fortunately for me, the machine also believed that I had no chance, and they didn't even bother to put up additional candidates to split what was clearly an anti-Fitzpatrick vote. So I got the race I wanted—one-on-one against Fitzpatrick. I believed that my main task was to let the public know there was a real campaign and that someone was running against Fitzpatrick. If I could do that, then I believed people would vote—not for me, but against him.

But with no money, how was I going to get that message out to a city of 1.6 million people? I decided I was going to go everywhere at all hours of the day and try to tell as many people as possible that I was running to "get rid of Fitzpatrick." And off I went. In February and March I stood on elevated subway platforms in 20-degree weather from 6:30 to 8:30 A.M. shaking hands and delivering the message to as many people as I could. I campaigned in markets, food courts, shopping centers, restaurants, indoor malls—anywhere I could find people. I didn't quit until midnight, after visiting three or four bars to catch the night crowd.

People think bars are bad places to campaign, but they really aren't. People are sitting around; they have time on their hands, and most are willing to talk to you. In fact, I'll never forget going into a place in Northeast Philadelphia called the Princeton Inn and meeting six or seven guys in their twenties who had a baseball record book on the bar. They said they would vote for me if I knew which Phillies player had hit the first home run in Veterans Stadium. Being a sports nut, I knew it was Don Money. Seven votes! For thirty-three years, I have never stopped campaigning in bars.

Once, when I was running for mayor, I stopped in a bar three days before the election. A TV crew was following me around that night. As I started to go toward a booth, the man sitting there jumped up and got in my face. I feared he was someone I had prosecuted, but he whispered to me, "Mr. Rendell, I'm gonna vote for you, but I'm not with my wife tonight. I told her I was working late and if she sees me with another woman on the eleven-o'clock news, I'm cooked." I dutifully turned and went to the other side of the bar. He was a real wuss, but I took a dive to preserve marital bliss.

I continued to go anywhere I could and anywhere I got invited. A friend garnered me an invitation to speak at a Sunday morning Synagogue Men's Club brunch. I gave an impassioned speech and then answered questions. A man asked me, "Mr. Rendell, are you Jewish?" I said I was, but I didn't want anyone there to vote for me for that reason, but rather because of the changes I wanted to bring about in the criminal justice system. After I finished, I ran into two young members in the parking lot and they told me, "You made a great speech and we're going to vote for you, but we would have even if you didn't . . . because you're Jewish!"

Ethnic voting is prevalent, not just in Philadelphia, but also around the nation. Even though the majority of Greeks are registered Republicans, they voted more than 95 percent for Mike Dukakis in 1988, as did African Americans in 2008 for Barack Obama.

The clearest evidence of ethnic voting patterns involved the election of a very fine Japanese American judge named William Marutani. I was helping the judge and we told him and his staffers that they should not put any posters with the judge's picture up in the five South Philadelphia wards that have mainly Italian American voters. He followed our advice and came in first in all five wards out of twenty-two candidates.

My plan to campaign everywhere, eighteen to twenty hours a day, was making headway, but not enough. I still wasn't building enough name recognition. Our fund-raising efforts were going nowhere. I would sit for four hours a day phoning lists of contributors to other Democratic campaigns. No one would ever take my calls. They were all afraid of the mayor and under no circumstances wanted to be involved on my campaign finance reports, which are publicly filed. My typical call would go something like this:

"Hello, is Mr. Jones there? It's Ed Rendell calling." The secretary would ask me to hold for a few seconds and later come back on the phone and say, "No, I'm sorry. Mr. Jones is in Florida [or Puerto Rico or Jamaica or Hawaii]." After four hours of this, day after day, I would come home and tell my wife, Midge, that we weren't raising any money, but I sure as heck was helping the travel business.

I also decided to try to raise money from my classmates at the University of Pennsylvania. After all, it had been just a little over ten years since we graduated, and I had been popular in school (I was the vice president of the student government). I had always heard that one of the benefits of going to an Ivy League school was the contacts you would make with classmates who would soon become leaders of business and industry. So I sent out a letter appealing for funds from my fellow Quakers (Penn's nickname) with great anticipation. I figured the money I would raise would easily finance a two- or three-week TV campaign.

What a rude awakening! The money the mailer brought in couldn't have bought a TV ad on a twenty-year-old *Godzilla* movie. I was crushed. I was especially disappointed in the response I received from Hedda Towler. Hedda, a Texan who went by the nickname "Peaches" during our school years, was a good-looking redhead. Though we never actually went out, we sort of flirted, and I always believed Peaches had a thing for me. Besides, there was a rumor that she came from Texas oil money. So when a response came in with the name Towler on the back of the envelope, I insisted on opening it myself. I was absolutely certain that it would contain a check for at least $10,000 and might even have one for a whole lot more.

As I tore open the envelope and pulled out the check, the first thing I saw was "10"—and my imagination ran wild. Then I took a closer look and was aghast to find that the check was for the grand sum of $10. So much for my sex appeal!! In truth, I really have gotten great support from my classmates over the years—Andy Kahn, Marty Baker, Pete Glazier, Pete Seigert, George Weiss, and others.

So in mid-March Midge and I made a fateful decision. We would borrow $10,000 and buy billboards all over the city. We didn't have a lot of money, so this was a big step. Back in 1977, $10,000 bought a hundred billboards for two months, from mid-March to mid-May. They weren't highway billboards, but they were in neighborhoods in every corner of the city. People would tell me that they drove past three of my billboards in a day. The boards were great. They had a picture of me with my tie down, wearing a vest (I never wore a vest), looking like Eliot Ness, a real tough, hard-nosed guy. They worked. They worked big-time! People began to get excited. We were attracting tons of volunteers. People began to realize that there was a real race.

I knew we were making headway when a councilman and ward leader, Jim Tayoun, from South Philadelphia came to see me. He told me to withdraw. I had impressed the organization and would be rewarded in the future, but I had no chance to win because his ward would beat me 5 to 1 and the other strong organization wards would do the same. He told me that I could not overcome those losses in other places. I thanked him but said I was going to hang in there.

Election Day, May 17, 1977, finally rolled around. All my enthusiasm and optimism vanished. I spent the day visiting polling places, and the organization committeemen were handing every voter material for Fitzpatrick. I will never forget visiting a polling place at a public housing high-rise. The committeeman was handing the residents a card with numbers on it, representing the ballot positions of the candidates. They didn't even give the residents the dignity of putting names on the cards. I asked my poll watcher if he thought we had any votes and he said, "Well, a priest and a nun came in and refused to take the card, but they looked Irish, so they probably voted for Fitzpatrick."

Well, the people fooled us all. I did lose Jim Tayoun's ward by a margin of 5 to 1, but I won divisions in Northeast Philly and Center City by 343 to 7; 296 to 5; and 412 to 19. It was a landslide victory—69 percent to 31 percent. And I won that division in the public housing high-rise 84 to 26. So the residents took the card, nodded yes to the committeeman, and voted the way they wanted. If the people know what's at stake in an election, no political organization, no matter how strong, can tell them how to vote. In every election since, TV and other media have continued to erode even the best organization's control.

The next morning, the *Philadelphia Inquirer* had a cartoon based on the movie *Network* that depicted people opening their windows and yelling, "We're mad as hell and we're not going to take it anymore!" And they didn't. The election marked the beginning of the end of the Rizzo machine. The citizens of Philadelphia had spoken.

I learned another lesson from my victory: politicians read election returns. The morning after the election, I received a call from Senator Buddy Cianfrani, the powerful head of the Pennsylvania Senate. Cianfrani had been a target of the special prosecution's office for years. We never got him, but the feds did. (He eventually went to prison as a result of federal prosecution.) He was the most powerful man in the Senate, and he sold his influence and created a web of corruption. After congratulating me, he told me that the Senate would pass a bill giving the seven of us who had worked for more than two months without pay in the special prosecutor's office our back pay *with interest!* "Do you believe in magic?"

CHAPTER 3

"I Wear Blue, Take Me Too!"

I became district attorney riding that wave of anti-establishment feelings. People wanted change, and I gave it to them—an aggressive, no-plea-bargaining approach to violent criminals, a new rape unit with specially trained assistant district attorneys who handled only sexual assault cases, a career criminal unit that tried violent offenders who had two prior convictions for violence, even a special unit that investigated and tried police corruption and police brutality. The rape, career criminal, and police brutality units were firsts for the DA's office.

In addition to these changes, I publicly went after judges who gave out lenient sentences to violent offenders, going so far as including "the worst sentences of the month" in our office news-letter, which went out to community groups and the media. The judges hated it; the public loved it. The career criminal unit

and the rape unit were instant successes. I was wildly popular—
the new kid in town making one great innovation after another.

I felt confident about my early start in office. Everything was
going very well. Not only were the conviction rates and the length
of sentences soaring, but also we were really helping the victims
of crime have their day in court. I will never forget a letter I
received during my second year in office.

It was from a couple from Northeast Philadelphia. They
recounted how their fourteen-year-old daughter was coming home
from school when an older man pulled her into the woods and
brutally raped her at knifepoint. The next time they saw her was
in the hospital, and their letter explained how radically she had
changed. She went from the most happy-go-lucky girl in her class
to a complete recluse. "Mr. Rendell," their letter read, "when
she came home from the hospital, everything had changed. She
stayed in her room and cried and cried and cried. She wouldn't
go to school. She wouldn't talk on the phone to her friends.
Somehow, incredibly, she blamed herself for what happened."

The letter went on to say that three weeks after the incident, the perpetrator was arrested. The day before the hearing
their daughter met the assigned assistant DA from the rape unit,
Andrea Foulkes. The letter said, "Andrea Foulkes did a great job,
Mr. Rendell. She presented the case brilliantly. The offender was
convicted and received twenty-five years in prison. But more than
that, she worked and worked with our daughter. She developed
a terrific relationship with her. We had taken her to psychia-
trists and psychologists and they couldn't get through to her, but
Andrea kept working with her. She finally got through to her that
what happened wasn't her fault. Then there came a day when
we heard a strange sound from our daughter's room. It wasn't the
usual sobbing. She was talking on the phone with one of her girl-
friends, and all of a sudden we heard her laughing again. It was a
miracle—Andrea Foulkes gave us our daughter back. God Bless
you, Mr. Rendell, for starting the rape unit and God Bless Andrea
Foulkes."

I took the letter and wrote on top of it, "Andrea, You won't get letters like this representing General Motors!" I was hooked; at age thirty-five I knew I wanted to spend the rest of my life in public service. No amount of money could make up for the feeling that letter gave me.

Things were going great. According to other candidates' polls, my favorable ratings (more about the polls and approval ratings later) were more than 80 percent. And then MOVE happened.

MOVE was a renegade African American group of ten to twenty members who lived in a compound—one large house in Powelton Village in West Philadelphia. They called themselves a "family" and they surely lived by their own rules. They were vegetarians and had an unusual lifestyle. They all changed their last name to Africa and preached against technology, saying we should go back to our hunter-gatherer roots. They violated several city regulations, especially ones involving sanitation and noise levels. Their neighbors, who were mostly working-class African Americans, began a cacophony of complaints to the city. City inspectors went out to the site, but MOVE members rebuffed them and they could not get inside the fenced-in compound. The "family" got agitated by all this and began to threaten their neighbors and brandish weapons at them. Tensions escalated. Ultimatums were issued. On August 6, 1978, the police and Mayor Rizzo came to me to approve search warrants for the weapons that were brandished and arrest warrants for a slew of misdemeanor and minor felonies. I approved the warrants because they were legally sufficient, but I had real doubts that this dilemma had to be resolved by an armed assault. A couple of days before, I had gone out to the compound and tried to talk to some MOVE members into surrendering and facing what would have been minor charges that surely would have wound up with probationary sentences.

On the morning of August 8 the police carried out an armed assault after they tried and failed via bullhorn to persuade the MOVE members to surrender. Initially they tried to penetrate the heavily barricaded house with water cannons and tear gas, but when that failed an incredible firefight ensued, with both sides leveling hundreds of rounds at each other. Philadelphia Police officer James Ramp was killed and several other policemen and firemen injured. Eventually, after they ran out of ammunition, the MOVE members surrendered.

This all took place early in the morning, and I thought it was all over. I was thinking about how we would try this homicide-conspiracy case against all MOVE members who were charged. Then, like a lightning bolt, came the news that a TV crew positioned high in a building behind the MOVE house had captured on tape the arrest of Delbert Africa, who had surrendered with his arms stretched out, forming a straight line. His hands were open and it was clear he was unarmed. Nevertheless, the police, inflamed over the death of Officer Ramp, proceeded to savagely beat him with rifle butts to the head and continued beating and kicking after he had fallen to the ground helplessly.

A firestorm was created. The beating of Delbert Africa became almost as big a story as the siege of the house and the death of Officer Ramp. And, of course, we were in the middle of both.

Prosecution of the MOVE members went forward. The evidence was overwhelming. The hearing and trial were circuses because the MOVE members did everything to disrupt the proceedings. Eventually they were tried in absentia.

As to the officers who beat Delbert Africa during his arrest, there was a diversity of opinion in our office. Most of the assistant district attorneys who worked on the same side as the police every day felt the beating was justified or excusable because the officers had just seen their fellow officer shot and killed. They simply weren't objective. They supported their "teammates." That's the very reason why I created a separate police brutality unit—assistant district attorneys who did not work with the police so they could be impartial and objective.

The lawyers in the brutality unit, led by their brilliant chief, George Parry, wanted us to issue an immediate arrest warrant. I was the final arbitrator, and I saw merit to both sides of the argument. I can imagine the anger and fury those officers felt against the killer of their comrade. Their loss and their pain were still fresh, and their minds and judgment had to have been clouded. But, on the other hand, they are trained professionals who have been taught to respect the justice system. And the law is clear: police cannot act as judge and jury and mete out punishment by themselves.

However, I wasn't sure that ordinary citizens, who would be the jury, would agree with me. I wanted to test how they would react to the circumstances of the siege, to the death of Officer Ramp, and to watching the videotape of the beating of Delbert Africa. So I decided to impanel a grand jury of ordinary citizens. Normally, grand juries do whatever the DA advises them to, but with this one we were careful not to tip our hand so we could watch how they reacted. When they viewed the tape of the beating, they reacted with horror and disgust. Based on that, I decided it was worth the inordinate expense of trying these officers before a jury. The grand jury indicted them based on our okay.

The indictment set off a furor and a raging controversy. Almost everyone was against charging the officers, something like 100 percent of the white population and more than 50 percent of African Americans. I knew that this would be the reaction. Before the indictment, my popularity was at an all-time high. There was strong talk of drafting me to run for mayor. To tell the truth, I was certain it was the right thing to indict the officers and uphold the law, but I was also scared about the reaction. I didn't know the half of it.

The day after the indictment, nearly a thousand police officers, many still in uniform, marched from City Hall to the Roundhouse (police headquarters) to our office building shouting, "I wear blue, take me too!" In a poll taken three days later by one of the potential mayoral candidates, my favorability rating had dropped 20 points, from 81 percent to 61 percent. I wasn't happy, clearly, but I hoped that when the reaction calmed I would bounce back. Guess what? It did! In a poll a month later, I was back to 75 percent.

At trial, the judge took the case away from the jury and, unbelievably, acquitted the defendants. Because of the double jeopardy provision, we could not even appeal.

I learned two lessons from this, which have guided me through my subsequent thirty-two years in politics. First, don't pay attention to polls. Definitely don't let poll numbers influence your policy decisions. If you do, you might as well quit. You were elected to make your own decisions, and sometimes those will not be popular. Sometimes your experience and training tell you something that goes counter to the public's gut reaction. Deal with it! When confronted by polls and my own occasional plummeting favorability ratings, I often think about Abraham Lincoln. Now considered to be one of our greatest presidents, he was so unpopular at the beginning of his third year as president that many believed he had no chance to be reelected. If there had been polls and favorability ratings back in 1863, Abe's probably would have been about 10 percent. Fortunately there weren't any, and he stayed the course, won the war, and was reelected. Would Lincoln have let a bunch of campaign advisers and bad poll numbers push him into letting the country be divided into two separate nations just so he could keep his job for an extra four years? No way! Abe would have laughed off those ratings and done what he believed was right for America's future. But would a lesser man have done so? Who knows? Thank God Lincoln had the courage of his convictions.

Second, and most importantly, remember that most people do not base their opinion of you on one decision. (And if they weigh one event heavily, it's usually something just before election day anyway.) Even if they disagree with you on an issue, if they believe you have guts and are a strong leader, they will support you regardless of their disagreement. Senator Russ Feingold is probably the best-known example of that. He spent three terms representing Wisconsin in the US Senate. During that time Wisconsin was a true swing state (like my own state), with members of both parties regularly winning statewide elections. Feingold managed to stay popular for years not by sticking to the middle of the road but by sticking to his principles. He was one of the most liberal members of the Senate and often took stances against his own party; he was the sole senator from either party to vote against the Patriot Act. He was never afraid of taking unpopular stances because his constituents knew he was doing what he thought was best for them. He lost his seat, as so many did, during the disastrous (for Democrats) 2010 midterm elections, but he kept it close until the end by being the same man he's always been. And when he lost, he walked out the door with his head held high.

So do what you believe in and let the chips fall where they may. It's the best way to govern. It also happens to be the best way to live with yourself, the best way to have fun in your political career, and the best way to feel good about the hardest decisions.

CHAPTER 4

Only a Smart Jewish Lawyer Can Turn This City Around

My political career almost ended in 1987, when I lost my second major election in twelve months.

After completing two successful terms as district attorney, I had concluded that no matter how effective the DA's office was, it could only deal with a small portion of the problems affecting our society, and I wanted to do more. I didn't want to just keep dealing with the results of those problems, but rather go after the root causes of them.

I had come to realize that no matter how strong or effective the criminal justice system was, it dealt with problems after they had been created. Sure, a good criminal justice system could protect people—especially poor people, who are 85 percent of the victims of crime—by making sure violent offenders were convicted and taken off the streets for significant periods of time. However, we were powerless to combat the root sources of crime—poverty, poor education, joblessness—that turned people into criminals.

So I decided to run for governor. My opponent in the Democratic primary was Robert P. Casey, a former state auditor general, who had run for governor and lost three times. I campaigned hard and ran a good race but lost, 56 percent to 44 percent. Again I challenged the machine—the party endorsed Casey—but although I lost this time, I never let them intimidate me, and I felt good about what I did. In the end, the voters made the right decision. I was too young, too inexperienced, and knew too little about the practical side of state government. Bob Casey was the right man at the right time, and he went on to be a fine governor, despite battling severe health challenges. He was anything but a wuss, which helped make him effective. He had great faith, and when he believed he was right, no risk scared him.

The day after I lost there was speculation that I would run for mayor of Philadelphia. The incumbent Democratic mayor, Wilson Goode, was responsible for the tragic bombing of another MOVE family compound, which resulted in the death of adults and children. The fire spread and demolished an entire city block. Even worse, the city was totally mismanaged, had a record deficit, and was on the brink of financial collapse.

A large number of business leaders came to me and said I had to run to save the city. I was psychologically wounded from my first loss ever in politics and vulnerable to flattery. So I said "yes." It turned out to be a terrible decision. First, because my heart wasn't in it. Despite his faults, Wilson Goode was a very decent man (and he has turned out to be a spectacular ex-mayor), and I liked him. Second, I had always had a great relationship with the city's black community, and I had no stomach for being the "white" candidate in a black-white Democratic primary contest against Goode.

When your heart isn't into a campaign, don't run! Voters will sense it immediately. I fell behind in the polls, and the same business leaders who urged me to run abandoned me and went back to supporting Goode. I learned another powerful lesson: never count on business leaders. Most of them, when it comes to politics, are wusses. They do care about big issues and change, but in the end, they will always be too afraid of offending the powers that be, even when those powers are dead wrong, to seriously take them on.

Needless to say, I got clobbered on election night and, worst of all, I won less than 3 percent of the African American vote. The experts said that these two losses spelled the end of my career. I thought so, too. I campaigned for Wilson Goode in the general election, not because I thought it could resuscitate my terminally ill political career, but because it was the right thing to do. Goode's opponent was the notorious Frank L. Rizzo, seeking a third term, who would have been an even worse mayor.

As it turned out, Goode won by less than seventeen thousand votes, and African Americans never forgot the efforts I made on Goode's behalf.

In politics, as in life, the world loves winners and outright shuns losers. I went back to practicing law and trying to raise enough money to pay off my campaign debts, including a second mortgage taken out on our shore home. Good luck! People would actually cross over to the other side of the street when they saw me coming, because they thought I would ask them for money. Lose two elections in twelve months and you find out who your friends are, and there aren't a whole lot of them. I could barely raise $100, but one day a check for $5,000 came in the mail from Leonard Tose, the owner of the Philadelphia Eagles, with a note that read, "Hope this helps. You did the right thing in running. Hang in there and don't get discouraged." I barely knew Leonard, but I never forgot his kindness, and when he fell on hard times near the end of his life, it gave me great joy to be in a position to help him.

Well, I settled into my routine at the law firm. Every once in a while someone would write an article about the 1991 mayoralty race. I was always mentioned, but immediately written off as a two-time loser, a hopeless also-ran. Everyone had counted me out, but the embers still burned deep in my heart. So I assembled a small crew to begin helping me prepare for 1991. It was a motley crew: Charlie Breslin, Thomas Carter, Donna Gentile, and Walter Watson. Charlie and Thomas became lifelong friends; Donna and Walter worked for me during my tenure as mayor. We started to get some speaking engagements and were doing a lot of research and fact-finding. Some days were good and some were more discouraging. The year 1988 turned into 1989 and then 1990, and it was getting close to decision time for me.

I was sincerely torn. On the one hand, I hadn't lost my desire to serve. I still thought I had something to contribute and could help turn Philadelphia around. On the other hand, I didn't want to lose another high-profile election and subject myself, Midge, and our son, Jesse, to the derision and abuse that come with that. And besides, I wasn't sure I really had a chance to win. The experts said no white candidate could ever win a Democratic primary again. African Americans now made up more than 50 percent of registered Democrats in the city. But I wasn't so sure that I didn't have a chance. The city was approaching bankruptcy, services were falling apart, jobs were leaving the city in droves, crime was rising, and all this was occurring even though the city had raised taxes nineteen times in the previous eleven years. I had a hunch that all Philadelphians—black or white—knew the city needed new, bold leadership and that that fact would override even racial voting patterns.

By March 1990, I knew I had to decide soon. If I were to run, I needed to start raising money almost immediately. I agonized over it until one night I was coming home (Midge and Jesse were away), and I stopped at a cheesesteak place close to our house. I placed my order and stood back to wait. I saw an older lady also waiting for her order. She looked Irish, somewhat disheveled, and almost toothless. She kept staring at me and finally she said, "Are you Rendell?" I said that I was. She then asked, "Well, are you going to run for mayor?" I was surprised and replied, "I don't know. What do you think?" She paused and thought about it for a little while, rubbed her chin, and then said, "You have to. This city is so fucked up that only a smart Jewish lawyer can turn it around."

I was juiced! If this little old lady understood that the city was in such bad shape that it needed someone smart to turn it around, then I had a chance. I had a real chance to win! The next morning, I told everyone I was running. I was off to the races and I never looked back.

The campaign was a whirlwind. I had four opponents in the primary, three black and one white. I had decided that if this was going to be my last campaign, I was going to go down telling people what they needed to hear, not what they wanted to hear. That strategy worked to a tee; people were desperate and they were ready to hear the truth. The key moment in the campaign came in the first televised debate. A question was asked of the five of us, "Would you be willing to take a strike to get the city's labor costs reduced to a level that will help eliminate the deficit?" The city's municipal unions were very powerful and had dominated Democratic politics for decades, but the city simply could not eliminate the deficit without significantly reducing labor costs (the city was paying 56 cents in benefits for every $1.00 in salary). I was lucky to be the last candidate to answer. My four opponents, all good men, hemmed and hawed and refused to give a direct answer. They wussed out. When my turn came, I didn't hesitate. I said, "Absolutely! If it takes a strike to get our labor costs under control, I will take one. We can't get out of this mess without significantly reducing them." At that moment, the race ended. The people wanted a candidate with the guts to do whatever was necessary—including taking on the unions to turn the city around. I received 51 percent of the total vote. My nearest pursuer got 28 percent.

The general election turned out to be easier than we anticipated. Frank Rizzo, the Republican candidate, passed away in July of a heart attack and his replacement never raised enough money to make it a race.

So I won. I was back! But what had I won? I was taking over as mayor of the city that faced the worst deficit (in percentage of its revenue) of any city in American history. It seemed to be a mission impossible, but I was ready. I hadn't stood out on all those el stops in the winter, worked twenty-hour days, and faced the abuse from being a two-time loser to waste the opportunity to turn the city around. I believed I could do it or we would go down trying. I resolved to do the necessary things even if they were unpopular. I was mentally and emotionally prepared to be a one-term mayor if that's what it took to fix the city.

I was so sure we would do what was right that I agreed to let Buzz Bissinger, a Pulitzer Prize–winning writer, spend the next three years sitting in on every meeting I had so he could chronicle our fight to save the city. People thought I was crazy. My good friend Rich Daley, the great mayor of Chicago, when told what I had agreed to do, said, "He did *what*?!"

Buzz went on to write a great book on the challenges facing all American cities, *A Prayer for the City*, and we succeeded in turning the city around way beyond my wildest dreams.

CHAPTER 5

The Truth about Waste, Fraud, and Abuse

The 2010 elections swept an array of Republicans into governors' offices in many blue states that had voted for President Obama just two years earlier. States such as Ohio, Michigan, Pennsylvania, and Wisconsin. All of those governors inherited significant budget problems due to the precipitous decline in state revenue caused by the recession and the loss of stimulus funds that had come from the federal government for the previous two years. These deficits made budget cuts inevitable, and budget cuts mean wage freezes and givebacks from public employee union members.

In some states — Indiana, Ohio, and Wisconsin — Republican governors extracted these concessions from their public unions (as did Democratic governors in New York and California), but with the help of Republican-controlled legislatures, they also went after the right of public employees' unions to bargain collectively. The effort in Wisconsin drew the most national attention when newly elected governor Scott Walker sought legislation that would have basically emasculated collective bargaining not only for state worker unions but also for county and municipal employee unions. This led to huge protest rallies and fourteen Democratic senators fleeing the state for weeks, denying the Senate the quorum it needed to enact Walker's plan. Eventually Walker prevailed, the legislature passed the bill, and he signed it into law.

Governor Walker (and some other Republican governors) contended that collective bargaining by public unions was the cause of the budget deficits they faced. That contention is patently ridiculous. First, if that were true, then Texas, a right-to-work state that has no public unions, would have no deficit; instead it has one of the largest in the nation. Second, though overly rich public employee contracts may be contributing causes to the states' deficits, they pale by comparison as a factor to the recession-caused loss of revenue and the withdrawal of federal stimulus funding.

All the anti-union bills signed around the country were written with the goal in mind of eliminating major donors to Democratic campaigns. And you wonder why these unions don't support Republicans, right?

Governor Walker and his brethren would also have you believe that states or municipalities can never prevail over public unions in collective bargaining negotiations. That is simply not true. What is true is that many governors and mayors have inexplicably given away the store during collective bargaining in an effort to keep labor peace. A lot of other times, both sides wussed out and signed agreements that kicked the can down the road, making it someone else's problem. But it doesn't have to be that way. I'm a perfect example that it doesn't.

I was inaugurated as the 121st mayor of Philadelphia on January 6, 1992. After being sworn in I gave an inaugural speech in which I laid out a road map that I believed Philadelphia had to follow if it was to escape bankruptcy and turn its future around. At the time we believed that the city faced at least a $250 million cumulative deficit. These days, with federal talk of billions and trillions coming and going, that doesn't sound like much. But at the time that was more than 12 percent of the city's annual budget ($2.3 billion). Worse still, it had raised taxes nineteen times in the eleven years before I was sworn in, so increasing tax rates wasn't an option. I knew that our only choice was to radically cut the cost of running our government. But I believed we could do so without dramatically reducing services. I had a plan, but to execute it meant radically changing the way the city operated. I gave everyone that warning in my inaugural address. I said that the city's finances make "short-run sacrifices and pain inevitable." I called on our city unions to "break with standard operating procedure" and to cooperate with our plans to reorganize city government and to introduce privatization. I warned, "We have to break the rules on how cities are governed." The fight to bring fiscal sanity to the city and significantly change its past patterns garnered national attention from beginning to end.

As the kids would say, "Game on." Our plan to eliminate our deficit was relatively simple—first, we needed to cut out every nickel of waste, save money by increasing productivity and efficiency, and generate more revenue without raising taxes; and second, we needed to substantially change our contracts with our four public employee unions.

The first part turned out to be easier to achieve than most observers believed. Led by our brilliant chief of staff, David L. Cohen, and our newly created Office of Management and Productivity (OMP), led by a creative entrepreneur, Tom Knox, we were able to eliminate more than $2.2 billion in management cost savings and additional revenue (without raising taxes) over the eight years I was mayor through implementation of these initiatives.

Our process was simple. David and I had researched every cost-saving initiative carried out in other cities and states, went through every past Philadelphia city controllers' suggestions for waste reduction over the past decade and all of the things that I had talked about in my campaign. For example, in 1990, the year before the election, I went to visit Mayor Ed Koch of New York City. I knew him from a meeting we had had during my time as district attorney and liked and admired his style and willingness to do tough things. The mayor had asked a group of business leaders to investigate ways by which New York could save money, and it became known as the "Carey Report." I told the mayor I had read the report and had a few questions about it. He said, "You read the report, all of it?" I said that I had read every one of its nearly one thousand pages, and he replied, "My God, there aren't three people alive who have read every page." But there was gold in them there pages. We made similar visits to Chicago, Denver, and Michigan and found literally hundreds of good ideas there, too.

Immediately after the election, I asked the Chamber of Commerce to help us by pulling together a broad-based team of loaned executives into what became known as the Mayor's Private Sector Task Force. In the end, more than four hundred private-sector volunteers were organized into review teams that spanned six cross-cutting issues (such as information technology, where the challenges were not limited to any single department), as well as teams covering twenty-nine separate city departments. Each review team had a CEO liaison and then one or two team leaders. In some cases the review was "adopted" by an organization. For example, the University of Pennsylvania adopted the Fiscal Management Team and Andersen Consulting adopted the Information Technology Team. The entire effort was overseen by David Pingree, a former respected managing director of the city.

In the end, the Mayor's Private Sector Task Force identified nearly four hundred management and productivity initiatives to be considered by the city government (including many initiatives that we had identified in the four years preceding my election as mayor through our visits to other cities and states and research that continued during the campaign). In our first Five-Year Financial

Plan alone (which was issued just a few months after I took office in 1992), we identified more than two hundred management and productivity initiatives that were projected to generate $74 million in savings and additional revenues and to reduce base personnel costs by $112 million. Over the term of the plan, the annual management and productivity improvements were projected to grow to $187 million in FY96, with annual labor savings totaling $142 million that same year. Thus, in total, our initial Five-Year Financial Plan projected $579 million in management and productivity reforms savings and $508 million in labor cost reductions over the term of the plan.

Identifying management and productivity reforms was, in some ways, the easy part. Actually implementing them was a little more complicated. So this is what we did.

We gave every department the responsibility of carrying out identified management and productivity reforms for that department. David, who is the most competent person I have ever met, held weekly review sessions department by department to monitor what progress was being made in implementing them. Managers came to fear these sessions (David could be, and often was, an unrelenting taskmaster), but they almost always produced. Meanwhile, the OMP and the Mayor's Private Sector Task Force continued to work to find new ways to save, and the middle managers of the government, who had never been asked, were a treasure trove of great new initiatives.

Some of ours were simple. Take real estate. In 1992, the city rented a boatload of space in private buildings. No one had ever paid much attention to the rates we were being charged. But we did now. And what we discovered was shocking. Under the city's charter, contracts (including leases) with a term longer than one year had to be approved by the City Council. Because in the past relations between mayors and the City Council had been so hostile, the typical city government practice was to enter into one-year leases. These leases, however, tended to have "evergreen" renewal clauses—that is, the lease would provide that if thirty or ninety days before the end of the one-year term or any extension term, neither party gave notice to the other of an intention to terminate the lease, the lease would automatically renew for another year, and rent would escalate by a stipulated figure. Believe it or not, these types of evergreen leases—which sometimes led to ten-, fifteen-, or twenty-year lease terms—were deemed by multiple city solicitors as not requiring City Council approval.

What we discovered, however, was that many of these leases, with their automatic rent escalations, had generated rental payments that far exceeded the market. In the early 1990s, the Philadelphia real estate market was at a low ebb, and vacancies abounded. We found numerous city leases of real estate where the rental fee was two, three, or even five times the current fair market rent for that property. One startling example occurred in the first few months I was in office. David was visited by Tom Knox, who told him that part of the Department of Human Services was in a Class C (a charitable classification) office building on North Broad Street. The lease on that building was one of those "evergreen" leases, with rent escalation of 11 percent per year. That lease was scheduled to renew on July 1 at the startling rental rate of $36 a square foot—at a time when you could get all the space you needed in brand-new top-of-the-line Class A gleaming towers for $20 to $23 a square foot.

We quickly met and I told Tom to send the landlord a letter announcing our intention not to renew the lease. Tom asked where those workers would go on such short notice. I said I didn't care, that we could set up tents in the City Hall courtyard for them, but we were not going to pay $36 a square foot for office space that was worth less than $10 a foot. Tom seemed incredulous, but he said okay and sent the letter. Within a day, David received a phone call from the landlord (who happened to have been a pretty nice campaign contributor of mine). "How can you guys do this to me?" asked the upset landlord. "This space is in such terrible condition, I will never be able to rent it in this real estate market." David patiently explained that we would be happy to enter into a market-rate lease with the landlord and keep our city workers in that space. The net result was a four-year lease at $7 a square foot with no escalation during the term of the lease. Of course, the lease had to be approved by the City Council, but it was happy to do so given the attractive terms.

A few examples of other ways we cut waste:

- Closing two city-owned trash transfer stations at a savings of more than $1 million a year.
- Implementing an aggressive "civilianization" program in the Police Department (hiring civilians at lower pay rates than uniformed police officers to perform civilian functions), generating annual savings of $3 million.
- Centralizing fleet management operations under the auspices of a new Office of Fleet Management and using that to improve the efficiency of procurement, maintenance, and deployment of motor vehicles, generating savings of $6 million per year.
- Streamlining the Parking Authority organization structure (including laying off multiple ward leaders and committee people), generating savings of $2 million a year.
- Creating a Municipal Energy Office to oversee a dozen energy efficiency initiatives (such as using energy-efficient lightbulbs and seeking appropriate energy discounts), generating $9 million a year in savings.
- Creating an Office of Risk Management to oversee the city's insurance program, generating more than $1 million a year in savings.
- Implementing changes in the Mayor's Office of Information Services to improve the procurement and deployment of technology throughout the city government, generating more than $2 million a year in savings.

One thing you'll notice when you look at a list like this is how a lot of little things add up. Often, when politicians start talking budget cuts they decide to just do away with some useful program altogether. It sounds bold to say you're going to get rid of the Department of Education, but it's actually lazy. You don't have to figure out what they're doing right and wrong; you don't have to spend time sorting through spreadsheets and talking to experts. It's the difference between diet and exercise and losing weight by cutting off your right arm. The best example of this is when a politician promises to cut the budget by getting rid of "waste, fraud, and abuse." It is just rhetoric, and sadly, the press often lets them get away with it by not requiring those who promise budget cuts to specify which cuts they would actually make, and where.

One of the critical management and productivity initiatives we implemented was also one of the most controversial: competitive contracting. In a nutshell, I believed that injecting competition into the provision of certain city government services provided us with an opportunity and an incentive for city managers to enhance productivity and to develop a leaner and more efficient government.

During my term as mayor, our competitive contracting program, which was carefully overseen by David, resulted in decisions to contract out forty-six different city services. The results were immediate improvements in service, a reduction in the city workforce of more than a thousand, and savings of almost $40 million annually. For example, the expense of a new facility management contract covering the Municipal Services Building, the Criminal Justice Center, and the City's One Parkway Building was more than $1 million less than the internal cost would have been, yet the city was able to obtain a higher quality of service, including preventive maintenance to safeguard the city's capital investments in these renovated buildings.

There was a lot of fear about competitive contracting—fear that we would lay off thousands of employees, fear that good-paying union jobs would be converted to nonunion jobs, and fear that services would decline. None of these fears proved to be justified. Although we reduced the city workforce by more than a thousand positions, almost no city workers were laid off, as we were able to either find them other jobs within the city government or ensure that they were hired by the successful private contractor. We gave preference to *unionized* contractors in our competitive contracting process, so the employees of our private contractors were unionized (albeit by different unions than the municipal unions). And our experience across the board was that services improved.

There was another terrific positive to our competitive contracting program. In creating the program, I insisted that the municipal workforce always be given a fair opportunity to compete to hold onto the work. So all of our competitive contracting initiatives were open to the municipal workforce submitting its own bid. And, in fact, the last step in every competitive contracting procurement was to give the municipal workforce a "last look." In one particularly large bid involving sludge disposal in the city's Water Department, the private bid came in about $2 million lower than the existing city costs, but the municipal workforce was able to put together a proposal that would have saved us the same amount of money. The results were that we did not contract out the work, and the municipal workforce continues to perform that work today, at an increased efficiency level. That was actually my favorite competitive contracting initiative!

We also bridged our budget gap by generating more revenue. We did it in a number of ways:

- One of our biggest revenue enhancement initiatives related to refining our system for obtaining state and federal reimbursements for services being provided to abused, neglected, and dependent children through our Department of Human Services. Through smarter budgeting, better technology, and far more aggressive negotiations, we were able to generate well over $100 million a year in additional reimbursements and revenues for our Department of Human Services.
- We implemented a 911 user fee, which generated more than $11 million a year in additional revenues to the city.

- The city operated a network of community-based health centers and clinics throughout the city. When I took office, more than 75 percent of the patients treated at these district health centers were being treated free, even though many of them were eligible for medical assistance (Medicare or Medicaid). By putting in a system to allow eligible (but not registered) Philadelphians to register for medical assistance on site at the district health centers, we saved almost $10 million a year in our Department of Health.
- Philadelphia has a wage tax, which is applied to residents of the city regardless of where they work and to nonresidents of the city if they work within the city limits. Employers within the city are required by law to withhold Philadelphia wage tax from all their employees. But employers in the suburbs were not required to withhold from Philadelphia residents working in their businesses. For years, Philadelphia had argued to the state government in Harrisburg for an amendment to the state law to require suburban employers to withhold the wage tax. Thanks to literally ten visits to Harrisburg by David, and the leadership of then Senate majority leader Joe Loeper, a Republican from suburban Delaware County, suburban withholding finally passed the Pennsylvania General Assembly in 1993. The net result to the city—an astonishing $25 million plus a year in additional tax revenues.
- We also revamped the city's fee structure. Most of the fees, for things like zoning permits or court filings, had not been adjusted for almost two decades. This initiative alone generated more than $5 million a year in additional revenues.

Our most effective way of generating new revenue was by collecting our taxes more effectively. During the campaign I said we could increase revenue by $15 million a year by doing a better job of collecting what was owed us, but the media scoffed at the idea. Well, we didn't generate just $15 million—we did $75 million a year for a couple of years and then more than $50 million a year going forward. One of the ways we accomplished this was by turning our past-due tax files over to private attorneys or collection agencies and giving them 18 percent of what they collected as compensation. It worked like a charm. One attorney earned more than $40 million, which means that he alone collected more than $200 million for us that previously would have been written off.

CHAPTER 6

"Fast Eddie, We Are Ready!"

All those initiatives I've been talking about were vital to our success in balancing our budget, but I knew that the mother lode was still renegotiation of contracts with Philadelphia's municipal unions. We had to freeze wages, reduce benefits, and change costly work rules.

I knew if we could change what we needed, we could eliminate the deficit, but to do so we needed to get the public on our side. So from the day I started my campaign to my first day in office I went everywhere, used every media outlet, to get across to the public how out of whack things were, how absurd some of our work rules were, and how the benefit structure our workers had was so much richer than they, the public working in the private sector, had. And everywhere I went, I stressed the reality that we were out of money and that we couldn't raise taxes anymore.

As we prepared for our union negotiations, David asked for a memorandum summarizing all the silly and unproductive work rules and practices that tied the hands of city managers. Joe Torsella, our brilliant deputy mayor for policy and planning, oversaw this project and prepared an amazing seventy-five-page memorandum. It was enough to make your head spin. Somehow the memorandum was leaked to the media, generating a number of stories, including one in the *Wall Street Journal* with the famous headline "How Many Workers Does It Take to Change a Lightbulb at Philadelphia International Airport?" (The answer, by the way, was four: an electrician to screw in the lightbulb, a laborer to carry the ladder and sweep up after the change, a carpenter to climb the ladder and unscrew the lightbulb, and a supervisor, who was required for every work crew of three or more employees.)

I was like a broken record and after about five months (the contract ran out on June 30) the press found a talking robot and sent it into my office. It was programmed so that no matter what you asked it, it always replied, "There's no money! There just isn't any money!" But that repetition was working. We were paying 56 cents in benefits for every $1 in salary (many prior mayors had given away the store). No private business could do that without going bankrupt (the private sector average in 1992 was 24 cents per $1 of salary), and we were hurtling toward bankruptcy.

Some of the benefits were simply absurd. In addition to negotiated vacation time, our workforce received fourteen paid holidays. This was extremely expensive, not only in lost productivity but also because those city workers who had to work on holidays (police, fire, EMTs, prison guards) received double-time pay. So each holiday cost us $7 million per year. I talked about this everywhere I went—"So for the emotional trauma of being away from their families on Flag Day, our workers get paid double time"—and in the end the new contract we negotiated reduced the holidays from fourteen to ten. Bingo: a yearly savings of $28 million.

Another major reform related to city workers' compensation and the disability system. I never wanted to deprive city workers who were legitimately injured on the job of fair disability payments and terrific health care. But our system was out of control. The stories of abuse were legendary. My favorite was probably the story of the city employee who slipped on a packet of ketchup while playing pinball at lunch in an arcade. This employee ended up incurring tens of thousands of dollars of medical bills and ultimately received a full disability pension. We were able to negotiate and implement a fairly radical reform of the entire workers' comp and disability pension system. The net result was that our employees were well taken care of, but we were able to strip tens of millions of dollars a year of fraud and abuse out of the system.

The biggest monetary issue in the contract negotiations, however, related to employee health care. Each of the city's municipal unions ran its own health care plan, and the city ran a fifth plan, for nonunionized employees. In 1992 the city was paying a staggering $475 per employee per month for the unionized workforce (rates ranged as high as $561), which was 50 percent higher than the private-sector average and 25 percent higher than the city-administered plan, at $382. If the city was going to balance its budget, I knew that we had to bring down the cost of health care to a more affordable level—but I had no interest in depriving our city workers of terrific medical coverage.

We decided to issue an RFP seeking bids to provide comprehensive medical, dental, and prescription coverage for employees and their families, with a very modest copay by the employees. The result of a robust bidding process was a low bid from US Healthcare for $194 per employee per month, which was 60 percent lower than what we were currently paying for our municipal workforce.

In the negotiations, we gave the unions a choice. They could give up their own health plans and allow us to accept the US Healthcare bid, or they could keep their health plans but accept the level of reimbursement comparable to the cost of the US Healthcare bid. While it was the most contentious issue in the negotiations, we were ultimately able to convince separate police and fire arbitrators, and then the blue- and white-collar unions, to accept a reduction in reimbursement that averaged nearly $100 less per employee per month, generating savings of almost $100 million a year. Our nonunion municipal workers, however, retained terrific health care plans that were the envy of their counterparts in the private sector.

As important as these benefit changes were, just as costly were a series of ludicrous work rules that previous contracts had given the workforce. Mayors always concentrated on the direct cost items—wages and benefits—and ignored work rules, giving in to whatever the unions asked for. We didn't. Again we talked about the most absurd ones all across the city. And in the end, we were able to wipe out most of the efficiency-crippling work rules and all other inefficient past practices from the new contracts.

Our public information campaign was working, but it wasn't an easy road to success. The unions fought back. Everywhere I went was picketed. Every press conference I held I was drowned out by union hecklers. My car was bumped and jostled. There were demonstrations and rallies against us. Remember, I was a Democratic mayor of a Democratic city, a Democrat who had run for governor, and I had to continually face the question of whether upsetting unions was the best thing for the city. The big rally was in May, when thousands of demonstrators ringed City Hall, chanting, "Fast Eddie, we are ready!" and carrying signs with pictures of David, Tom Knox, and Alan Davis that read, "These men want to pick your gynecologist."

The pressure for us to fold and give the unions what they wanted came not only locally but from national labor leaders as well. In the summer of 1992 I attended the Democratic National Convention in New York City. Of course, I sat with the Pennsylvania delegation, and throughout the four days we were visited by AFSCME union members from virtually every state asking me how I, as a Democrat, could be so mean to union workers. I patiently (not my strong suit) explained that we were out of money and I was just trying to save our workforce's jobs. I didn't mollify any of them and it made for an extremely tense and tiring four days.

A few months later, the head of the national AFL-CIO asked if he and other heads of international unions could come to Philadelphia and meet with me. I said sure, even though I knew what was coming. More than a dozen labor leaders from Washington, DC, met with me. I tried to explain our situation and that the changes in benefits and work rules I was seeking would enable me to balance our budget without laying off a single worker. They weren't interested—they wanted no givebacks, no concessions. They were interested in "running" the negotiations no matter what the cost. Their strategy was simple: to threaten and intimidate me. They told me, not too subtly, that I was a bright young man with a great future in national and state politics and it would be a shame if I blew it by becoming known as antiunion. But they were just wasting their time. I had promised the people of Philadelphia in that first debate that I would take a strike if it were necessary to turn the city around, and I wasn't going back on my promise to them. I guess I did okay anyway, although some of them never forgave me.

But in the end they weren't ready and we were. I knew the campaign we were waging would be successful one night in May when I was watching Jesse's Little League team play in the East Falls League playoffs. I was standing with the other dads of our team's players when the father of one of the other team's kids came over. He worked in the Philadelphia Water Department, and he started giving me grief about being too hard on city workers. The last thing I wanted to do was get into an argument over this at my son's baseball game. I didn't have to. The other dads, who were mostly building tradesmen, started yelling at the city worker about how they only get seven paid holidays, not fourteen, and how they didn't get their pensions when they turned fifty-five. My God, I thought: they are reciting chapter and verse what I had been saying for months. I knew at that moment that we would win. I knew there would be a strike, but that with no public support, the union would fold. There was a strike, it lasted seventeen hours, the union folded, and we negotiated and signed the most concessionary contract in city history.

The contract, won through the collective bargaining process, was the key to wiping out our deficit in eighteen months, which led to six straight years of economic growth and surpluses. It helped produce what the *New York Times* called "one of the most stunning turnarounds in recent municipal history."

Of course, in life, if you take on a task that is incredibly complex, thankless, or tiresome, and you do well with it, you get rewarded with more of the same. So it was that I found myself in January 2003 with, as Yogi Berra said, "déjà vu all over again." I inherited a state government with a whopping $2.3 billion deficit. As governor, I again had to reduce the cost of the operation of our government, and contract negotiations would be a significant part of it. Again, we succeeded beyond anyone's expectations. During the campaign I said we could reduce the cost of the operation of state government by $1 billion a year. Again the press scoffed and again we did more—we cut our costs by more than $1.75 billion per year. By 2010 the budget for our general governmental operations was less than it was in 2002. Not adjusted for inflation, but less in real dollars.

How did we do it? Just like in Philadelphia, we applied commonsense oversight to virtually every aspect of governmental spending.

When we arrived in the state capital of Harrisburg we found that although the state was spending more than $3.4 billion for goods and services, there was absolutely no attempt made to reduce that cost by leveraging the tremendous buying power of the state. I immediately put David Yarkin, our bright young deputy secretary of general services, in charge of what we called our strategic sourcing initiative. The results were stunning. By sourcing our purchasing, in four years we saved $320 million on the cost of providing goods and services.

We saved money by putting all agency purchasing under one contract. So all computers bought were from one vendor, all furniture, all telephone services (e.g., all cell phones), and so forth.

The most glaring example of the need for sourcing our purchasing was in office supplies. The various state departments and agencies purchased their supplies separately from more than two thousand unique suppliers! The state had seventeen warehouses in Harrisburg, almost one for each department. For pens for the Erie revenue office, the vendor delivered them to the Harrisburg warehouse, which, in turn, shipped them to Erie. We put all our office supply needs out to bid for one vendor. We wound up saving $14 million annually and were able to reduce the number of state warehouses from seventeen to four. The vendor delivered directly to the various state offices around the commonwealth.

Another example was the savings we achieved in our medical assistance program (Pennsylvania's unique system for helping the elderly and the disabled with medical benefits beyond any federal help they may qualify for). Without reducing any needed benefits, we were able to reduce our spending on medical assistance by $500 million per year. We did so by controlling our pharmaceutical purchasing, by cutting down on the purchase of unneeded durable medical equipment, by renegotiating rates with our providers, and by increased oversight of our fees for service programs, which reduced usage.

The savings in our contract—again achieved by winning the collective bargaining process—were also a key part of our incredible success in reducing the cost of government.

This time I didn't need to educate the voters about our dire budget circumstances. The state budget deficit of $2.3 billion set the stage for us to take a hard line in our negotiations with the unions. It's a good thing we did, because doing so saved us $1.3 billion during my first term as governor. We signed a four-year contract that froze wages for the first two years, with a 3 percent increase in the third year and a delayed 3.5 percent increase in the final year.

The contract also eliminated service-based salary step increases in the first year for the first time in the history of the commonwealth.

But we didn't stop there. On top of historically low annual wage increases, the contract mandated the first-ever employee contributions to their own health care coverage. New hires immediately began to pay for their health care based on a percentage of their wages, as well as for dependent coverage for the first six months and for more costly plan options. Existing employees also started to make a contribution at the same rate two years later. Breaking this barrier saved us $270 million over my eight-year tenure.

To sweeten the deal for the union and to test an innovative way to drive down health care costs, that contract launched an intensive employee wellness program. For employees who opted to participate, they could pay a reduced premium toward their health care. Of course, collecting less from the employee could have meant the state would have to pay more. But we bet on the program working, and we were right—by getting employees to focus on their own health and wellness, we were able to maintain modest growth in medical claims of less than 7 percent, as compared to double-digit growth in other health plans.

I took our cost-cutting approach to union benefits beyond the contract. Union retirees had a Cadillac health care package. Because the commonwealth had the right to modify retiree health benefits, I could reform the benefits and drive down costs, bigtime. But exacting savings from this health care package was not without political risk, since changes to this package would affect more than 60,000 current retirees and portend a less robust retiree health package for every one of the 167,000 currently employed state workers. In the face of mighty opposition, we restructured this health care package to make several important changes, including the introduction of new retiree cost-sharing, increasing the years of service eligibility to qualify for benefits, and changing the benefits themselves. As a result, Pennsylvania taxpayers paid $365 million less than they were paying in retiree health care costs over my eight years as governor and continue to pay less every year.

So to Scott Walker and all the Scott Walker wannabes out there, you're wrong. Collective bargaining doesn't produce deficits. Mayors and governors who give away the store do. The collective bargaining process doesn't always mean that the unions win. There are plenty of other mayors and governors who did what I did—dug their heels in, took their case to the people, and saved the costs necessary to protect their taxpayers.

CHAPTER 7

What's a Nice Jewish Boy Doing Holding Hands with Louis Farrakhan?

I woke up on the morning of April 16, 1997, to find out that my fears had been realized. The front page of the *Philadelphia Daily News* had a picture of me and Louis Farrakhan, the leader of the Nation of Islam, holding hands on a church dais. We were with several other religious leaders, but it was Farrakhan I was holding hands with.

How did this happen? How did a Jewish mayor wind up holding hands with a Muslim leader who, as the *Daily News* wrote, "is widely regarded as anti-Semitic"? How did I manage to get myself on the very short list of publicly elected officials to share the stage with him?

It started in the Grays Ferry section of Philadelphia when a mob of white men beat up an African American woman, Annette Williams, her son, and her nephew outside a Roman Catholic

Church social hall. Grays Ferry had been for a long time before then a powder keg of racial tensions. It had been predominantly white, but was becoming more integrated every year, causing tensions to rise. Eight men were arrested and charged with ethnic intimidation. A month later two black men shot and killed a sixteen-year-old white boy during a drugstore robbery. Racial tension began to boil over and reach a crescendo when local black community groups announced their intention to march through Grays Ferry to protest violence against blacks. Minister Farrakhan had announced his intention, and that of the Nation of Islam, to come to Philadelphia and join the march.

I knew that if he and many outsiders from the Nation of Islam joined the march it would dramatically increase both the number of marchers and the possibility that we could have a full-scale race riot on our hands that would do permanent damage to Grays Ferry and the entire city. That was especially true because two weeks later, the Presidential Summit on Volunteerism was scheduled to be held in Philadelphia, and a race riot might force its cancellation. All it would take was one person shooting a marcher, or even worse, Minister Farrakhan, to set off widespread violence and pandemonium.

At the urging of local African American leaders and with the help of City Council president John Street and local Muslim leader Minister Rodney Muhammad, I agreed to write Minister Farrakhan and ask him not to join the march but to participate in a rally against racism that local leaders from government and clergy would attend at a local church. Minister Farrakhan agreed to call off his and the Nation of Islam's participation in the march if I would join the church service.

I agreed, and immediately my decision was blasted by the Board of Rabbis of Greater Philadelphia and by the Anti-Defamation League as well as many other Jewish groups. I knew that these would happen, but I never hesitated. I realized that my responsibility as mayor to try to avoid a potentially damaging race riot far outweighed my responsibility or personal feelings as a Jew. I could take a hit on my popularity if it meant holding the city together.

The plan worked like a charm. The march went on but instead of having five thousand or more participants it had only five hundred, none of whom was an outsider from the controversial Nation of Islam. There were no serious incidents at the march. The rally, at Tindley Temple United Methodist Church, was packed, with more than three thousand people inside and another thousand listening on speakers outside. It was going great. My remarks were well received by the mostly African American audience, and Minister Farrakhan's speech was terrific, not incendiary in the slightest. The *New York Times* reported it well:

> Mr. Rendell became one of the few big-city mayors ever to share a podium with Mr. Farrakhan, a circumstance that was all the more unusual because Mr. Rendell is Jewish and Mr. Farrakhan is widely regarded as anti-Semitic. Representatives from the city's leading Jewish and Roman Catholic organizations were invited to participate in the rally, but all declined. . . .
>
> Mr. Farrakhan praised Mayor Rendell, a popular Democrat, for "his courage and strength to rise above emotion and differences that might be between us or our communities." Mr. Farrakhan added: "I believe, Mayor Rendell, that history will applaud your efforts."

In my talk, I addressed the fact that Farrakhan was so controversial, and that it was unusual for me to share a stage with him like this. But if people who disagreed couldn't share a church podium, how could they share a city neighborhood? Farrakhan, for his part, suggested that this might be the beginning of a dialogue between him and prominent American Jews. It wasn't.

Farrakhan spoke for an hour and half, with the crowd following him the whole way. He railed against intolerance, saying it could doom America.

The minister was especially effective when he criticized the white men who attacked Mrs. Williams, but also black men who beat up black women with impunity. He did great; his speech was all I hoped for and then some. Then it happened. The presiding minister of the church asked us all to rise and join hands as we sang "We Shall Overcome." A terrific chill went up my spine. I was sitting between Minister Farrakhan and John Street and knew that there was no escape (though for a minute I thought about faking that I was fainting from the heat and that the tension was forcing me to leave the stage). So I decided to suck it up but I kept inching closer and closer to my good friend John Street, hoping that it was he and I who would be pictured together the next day.

No such luck, but in the end it was the right thing to do, and I would do it again. I suffered some short-term slings and arrows. But when I ran for governor five years later, despite the incident being raised against me, I received something like 93 percent of the Jewish vote.

Even if the result had been different and I had lost my reelection bid because of the picture with Farrakhan, I still would have had no regrets for having done it. Leaders get elected to lead, and that often means making decisions that are the right thing but that are very unpopular when you make them. If you are mayor, county executive, governor, or president it better be in your DNA to have the willingness to make correct but unpopular decisions. Wusses need not apply. Your job is to do what's best for—and to protect—the constituents you serve. It is not to protect your job. If all you do is play it safe and take no risks you'll be a terrible leader and you won't have a bit of fun, either.

When I was in my first year as mayor I got a call from a community activist who had been a big supporter from my first race for DA. He told me that if I followed through with the city's plans to put a supermarket in his neighborhood, his group would come down to City Hall and protest outside my office. I told him, only half-kiddingly, "Call me before you come down and I'll make sure you get a time slot. We have five to ten groups protesting us every day and I'll make sure we can fit you in."

The truth is that for years City Hall had been paralyzed any time ten people or more showed up with signs. It would stop development in its tracks—even if the development was slated to create 250 new jobs. Rina Cutler, one of the most competent people who has ever worked for me, served as my deputy secretary of the Pennsylvania Department of Transportation and, when I was mayor, as director of our Parking Authority (which she turned into a great development agency, using its bonding powers effectively). Rina expanded on the famous NIMBY phrase— "not in my backyard"—and coined a new one, BANANA—"build absolutely nothing anywhere near anyone"—and then another, NOPE—"not on planet Earth"—and finally, CAVE—"citizens against virtually everything."

We changed that big-time. When a group didn't like our plans, I met with them, listened to their concerns, and tried to ameliorate as many as we could. But very often we couldn't deal with all their objections and I finally had to tell them, "Look, we did as much as we could to alleviate the problems you raised, but we couldn't do everything you asked. So we are going ahead and if you want you'll get your chance to vote against me on November 7, 1995."

Very few of them did!

CHAPTER 8

"We Don't Cover Plane Landings!"

S now is the bane of a mayor's existence. That lovely white stuff, which looks so pretty when it first falls, is nothing but a financial headache for cities, because it can run up millions of dollars of overtime for the Streets Department. I'll never forget my first day as former mayor of Philadelphia. John Street had been sworn in as my successor on Monday. I awoke Tuesday and, as I always did, went to the window and opened the blinds, and saw that it was snowing heavily. That old familiar chill went up my spine, as it had for the previous eight years, and then a revelation hit me: "Not my job!"

I got reelected as mayor in 1995 with 81 percent of the vote and began my second term in January 1996. Within a few days, we got hit by a record-breaking snowstorm. I remember that it looked so beautiful as it came down. But in a few hours it turned fierce, and over the next thirty-six hours Philadelphia was pounded by thirty-three inches of snow.

Needless to say, that record-breaking amount of snow presented an incredible challenge for the Streets Department. But led by Joe Martz, our extraordinarily effective operations manager, they did a great job keeping our major arteries open and clearing secondary streets as well. Our biggest problem was what to do with this snow when we had cleared it. We couldn't stack it up on the curbs, as we normally did—there was just too much of it. We had no solutions. The easiest out was to dump it in the river, but we weren't allowed to do so by the EPA. The salt and chemicals used in snow clearing got into the snow, and that might pollute the river. We were desperate, so I made an executive decision, as I often did as mayor or governor. Because of the urgent circumstances and emergency conditions, I would issue an order that would violate the law but that would create a better outcome for the people I served. And besides, anyone familiar with the Schuylkill River would honestly tell you that a little salt could hardly make its pollution much worse.

Well, as soon as the snow stopped the two stations and newspapers sent out reporters to interview the public and ask them what type of job the city had done in clearing the snow. We had done a great job given the magnitude of the storm, and the people corroborated that to all the reporters. Almost everyone went with that as their story line, but not the *Philadelphia Inquirer*. They had dispatched a young woman reporter to interview people in the neighborhoods. She heard the same positive response and filed a story saying that. But her editor wasn't satisfied and told her to find some people who disagreed, so she could write a negative story saying that the city had screwed up. She was taken aback by this and recounted it to David Cohen. She was upset and had tears in her eyes as she told him.

David, outraged, called the editor and complained vigorously. The editor listened and responded tersely, "David, we don't cover plane landings!" Amazing and sad, but all too true. Good news about what government does—well, it's basically no news. It's rarely covered, and if it is at all, it's buried in the back of the paper or at the end of a newscast.

A good case in point involved what was the greatest controversy during my tenure as governor. In 2004, the legislature wanted a large increase in their pay, but I refused to accede to their demands. This created a great deal of friction, and they made the same demands in 2005. This time they made the passage of our agenda contingent upon my acceptance. I did so reluctantly, and it was a mistake that caused many legislators in leadership to lose reelection. After I signed the pay raise legislation, citizen outrage was immediate and intense. It didn't die out, either. It built to a crescendo, a veritable fever pitch fanned by every media outlet in the state. Not only did every paper editorially savage the pay raise (as they should have), but also the day-to-day coverage was nonstop.

About seven weeks later, I was in Wilkes-Barre, and after I finished my speech an elderly woman came up to me and began vociferously berating me for signing the pay raise bill. She poked me in the chest continually while she yelled at me. Finally she said, "And I wouldn't even mind the pay raise if you guys in Harrisburg ever did anything for me!" I took a chance and asked her if she was in our state's free prescription plan for seniors. She said "yes." Then I asked her how long she'd been enrolled and she replied, "Just a few months. I wasn't eligible before, because I had too much retirement income, but they raised the eligibility level, so I got in." I almost screamed at her, "Madam, who do you think 'they' is? You're looking at 'they.'" One of my first initiatives as governor was to expand our Pace program by significantly raising the income level for eligibility. At its height, that prescription drug program had 450,000 enrollees, but when I was elected we were down to 200,000 because the Social Security COLA kept increasing the seniors' benefit, which would raise the income level above the Pace threshold. By cost-saving initiatives and by allowing our lottery to generate added revenue, we have been able to almost double the amount of seniors eligible for free prescriptions.

I was furious that the lady didn't realize that I—one of those "Harrisburg guys"—was responsible for doing something that had actually changed her life for the better. But when I got back to the capital, I asked my press people to check the coverage the Wilkes-Barre daily had given our action that increased the eligibility for the Pace program. They wrote one story, and it was on page twenty-seven and contained sixteen lines. The same paper had news about the pay raise on its front page more than twenty times, and stories about it were written containing thousands of lines. Good news is no news these days, so it wasn't that lady's fault.

You might call it the Woodward and Bernstein fallacy. Ask anyone at a newspaper why they got into the business, and they're likely to mention the movie *All the President's Men*. It's a great movie about great reporting, but it leads many reporters to think that bringing down an elected official is the only path to glory. In fact, most Pulitzers are given out for explaining something important. Often it's for providing important updates and overviews of a complicated disaster. Even Woodward himself followed up his Watergate reporting with a shelf of best sellers that explained the inner workings of governmental institutions. None of them brought down another presidency.

Far too often reporters begin their investigations with a distinct conclusion in mind. The results are often unfair to the targets and, very often, bad journalism. It's not that reporters lie or editors allow falsehoods to get into print (or on the air). It's that they refuse to include in their stories any facts that cut against their story line, their initial conclusion.

Another good example of this involves campaign fund-raising in general, and mine in particular. Let me begin by saying that I am a very adept fund-raiser. In my four successful elections for mayor and governor, I set the all-time records for money raised for those offices. One day while I was mayor, Senators John McCain and Russ Feingold came to Philadelphia to hold a press conference touting their proposed campaign-financing legislation. They asked me to attend and endorse the bill. I did so because I thought it would be good for the country. Besides, it wouldn't affect me; it only applied to federal elections. We held the press conference and I made a spirited endorsement. The next day the *Philadelphia Daily News* wrote an editorial saying, "Ed Rendell endorsing campaign finance reform is like Ali Baba endorsing an end to thievery."

The fact that I raised so much money was like waving a red flag in front of a bull—the media simply assumed that anyone who raises that much money must be "selling" city or state contracts. Not so. I have never given a government contract to a donor unless that donor's bid was the best for the citizens. No one has ever disproved that assertion. Nevertheless, every time a campaign finance report was filed, some media outlet would run a story showing who my top ten donors were and what government business they received. Each time someone wrote or aired a story, they would interview me first. I would patiently demonstrate to them the incorrectness of their story line by showing them that in the three biggest contracts we had given out, the bidders who had contributed nothing or virtually nothing to my campaign were chosen over others who had contributed or raised hundreds of thousands of dollars. The reporters would all take notes or record me detailing this, but they would then file stories leaving it all out. Why? Because it disproved their basic story line!

A great example of this was my last appearance on *60 Minutes*. They wanted to talk to me about gambling in Pennsylvania. One of my media advisers, Dr. Kirstin Snow, told me not to do it because she intuited that the story line would be antigambling, and having the power to edit, they would cut anything good that I said to support why we had expanded gaming and only go with answers that supported their story line.

Despite her stern warning, I decided to do the interview. I did so because first I still had a slightly idealistic view of the press, especially the major networks, and I believed that they would be, to quote Fox, "fair and balanced." Second, I always believe I can charm or convince anyone of anything. And third, we had a great story to tell.

Prior to our legalizing gambling, a study had shown that 1 million of our 12.4 million citizens leave the state every year to gamble away $4 billion from which Pennsylvania gets no benefits, no taxes. Since they were going to gamble anyway, I decided that they should gamble here so we could use the tax revenues to reduce or eliminate property taxes, especially for our seniors. It worked to a tee. Tax revenues from gaming topped $1.3 billion — the most revenue of any state in the nation — and we were able to reduce property taxes across the board and eliminate them for 125,000 senior homeowners.

I tried to make that point once the show taping began, but the producer kept prompting the reporter, Lesley Stahl, to ask over and over again about the supposed harm it creates. I explained that not legalizing gaming in Pennsylvania would not stop those citizens who wanted to gamble because there were so many options in nearby states, especially New Jersey. But they kept asking me the same question over and over. I finally snapped and blew up on camera, calling the producer a "simpleton." Needless to say, that was the clip that was used as the program teaser and shown on the air, and it looked like I was having a meltdown. Sadly, I was wrong about 60 Minutes. They never were interested in portraying the truth about gambling in Pennsylvania, only the downsides. And worse, I was wrong not to follow my adviser's advice. Sometimes you are not the smartest person in the room.

CHAPTER 9

"Harper Valley PTA"

In January 1992, my first month as mayor, a former mayor of Little Rock, Arkansas, Lottie Shackelford, introduced me to the governor of her state, Bill Clinton, at the U.S. Conference of Mayors' meeting in Washington, DC. After talking with him for fifteen minutes, I fell in love—and through the good and the bad of the next twenty years I have never fallen out of love. I know he is a flawed person (aren't we all?) and, for an incredibly smart individual, he had some of the worse lapses of judgment you could ever imagine. But he was a very good president—and could have been a great one absent those lapses—who did great things for the American people and cared very much for the challenges and hardships that the ordinary person faced. When you talk to him, he makes you feel that you are the only person in the world. Cynics say it's phony, but it's not. I have seen

Bill Clinton go to incredible lengths to help people. Not the machers or the very rich and powerful, but ordinary citizens in desperate need. That caring and passion to fight injustice are what has made Bill Clinton a truly great ex-president and what drives the Clinton Foundation to do so much good and to alleviate so much suffering throughout the world.

Bill Clinton was, and still is, a policy wonk. It's hard to believe that someone so charismatic cares so much about the minutiae of complex policy matters, but he does and is such a great quick study that he masters those details almost instantaneously. At our second meeting, riding in a car in Philadelphia, when I had yet to commit to endorsing his candidacy, he blew me away with his almost encyclopedic knowledge of the problems facing American cities and the vital need to revitalize the nation's infrastructure (a lifelong passion for me as well). I was hooked and decided I would do everything I could to help him become president.

Like many Clinton supporters, I was rocked by the Gennifer Flowers revelations. Not because I thought it went to Clinton's fitness for the presidency, but because I believe it spelled doom for his chances in the New Hampshire primary. I will never forget the Saturday night before the primary, I was at a Sons of Italy dinner in Philadelphia and I was sitting next to the Italian ambassador to the United States. He was a charming, urbane, and sophisticated man and we were having an interesting conversation when he asked, "Mayor, I mean no offense, but what is wrong with your country? I read about the trouble this young governor is in because of an affair. In my country, it would help him, because the voters would consider it a sign of his vitality and energy." Six years later, I thought about the ambassador when the Monica Lewinsky scandal broke.

The voters of New Hampshire surprised everyone and made Bill Clinton the "comeback kid." He was off to the races and never looked back until he was nominated at the Democratic National Convention in New York City.

The Pennsylvania primary was pretty meaningless. It was held in late April, and by then Clinton had it wrapped up. The night before the primary, we had a fund-raiser for the Clinton campaign. Midge was out of town and I couldn't get a babysitter for Jesse, so I picked him up after Little League practice and took him to the dinner with me, so he could meet the future president and Hillary. I knew Jesse would not eat the chicken dinner we were to be served, so using the enormous power of the mayor, I called the hotel and ordered him a cheeseburger and fries. When the dinner came Jesse was sitting next to Governor Clinton, and was still dressed in his baseball uniform. I was seated next to Hillary. As dinner progressed and as Jesse dug into his burger and fries, Governor Clinton was pushing around his chicken with a notable lack of enthusiasm, all the while casting covetous eyes at Jesse's plate. My twelve-year-old son was oblivious to the fact that the next president of the United States wanted to share his meal and he ate on, totally unaware. Even if he had noticed, however, there was no way he was going to share. Ah, the innocence of youth!

The fall campaign was much harder and the outcome almost always in doubt. Bill Clinton proved to be an incredible candidate. From retail campaigning to debating, there was no one better. It soon became clear that Pennsylvania would be one of the two or three key states in determining the outcome. I was resolute in driving the city turnout as high as possible to give him the winning margin. We did and the governor carried Philadelphia by three hundred thousand votes. He did better than any Democratic presidential candidate had in the Philadelphia suburbs and held his own in western Pennsylvania, once a Democratic bastion, but which was becoming increasingly conservative because of guns and abortion. But Clinton was able to defend concerns over the gun issue because he truly was an experienced hunter and could talk like one. This was true even when he ran for reelection in 1996, having authored the Brady Bill and the assault weapon ban. I watched with wonder when at a rally in Westmoreland County (near Pittsburgh) he told the crowd (with a hint of hillbilly twang), "The Brady Bill has stopped a half a million dangerous felons from getting guns and none of you have lost a minute in the deer woods!" He had them at "deer woods."

The late, great Ann Richards told a joke that crystallized the reason why Bill Clinton did well with hunters and Al Gore not so much. It's all about the lingo. Ann's story was set in 2000 and was premised on Clinton trying to help Gore with the hunters' vote. He took Al out and got him the right hunting duds and the right shotgun and then, properly clad and armed, they went out to a lake and knelt in a duck blind. While waiting, they saw a beautiful naked blond woman coming out of the water. She looked at them and said, "What are you doing, boys?"

Clinton replied, "We're hunting for game."

She rejoined, "Well, I'm game!"

So Gore shoots her!

You had to hear Ann tell it—with gusto and a Texas drawl.

During his presidency, Bill Clinton was a great friend to American cities, and he and Vice President Gore contributed mightily to the turnaround of Philadelphia. Their policies were designed to help cities in every possible way. And if there were other things they could do, they did them.

I'll never forget when I heard that in a cost-cutting measure the federal government was eliminating four of its ten IRS centers. One of those centers was in Philadelphia and employed more than four thousand workers. Our city was coming back, but we surely couldn't afford to lose that many jobs. So on the president's next visit to Philadelphia, I asked if I could ride in with him from the airport, which would give me fifteen minutes alone with him to plead my case. My request was granted.

When we got in the car, I told the president of my concern and then handed him a piece of paper with numbers on it. It read

9%	2%
20%	7%
81%	38%

The president asked what it meant. I told him it was a comparison between Philadelphia and Boise, Idaho (where one of the other ten centers was). With the Philadelphia percentage listed first, the first line was unemployment, the second was the poverty rate, and the third was the percentage of votes he had received in his election in each city, with an astounding 81 percent in Philadelphia. He looked at them and nodded. Case closed. The jury understood clearly. The IRS center is in Philadelphia today and is doing just fine.

President Clinton wasn't reluctant to turn the tables and ask for help, too. And not just on his elections, either. The crime bill was one of the president's major domestic initiatives, but it was defeated in the Senate by a few votes. I went to a Phillies game that evening and was enjoying myself when one of my security detail said I had a call from the White House. President Clinton wanted me and Mayor Giuliani—both of us big-city mayors and former prosecutors—to come to Washington for a press conference and then fly with him on *Air Force One* to St. Paul, Minnesota, to speak at a US Police Chiefs' convention. We were helping him launch a counteroffensive to try to get the bill passed into law.

Over the next two weeks, Rudy and I worked the phones and had some success. We persuaded enough senators to change their votes, and the crime bill became law. I will always remember the conversation I had with that great progressive Republican icon John Chafee of Rhode Island. It was an honor for me to even speak to him, let alone help change his vote.

Six months after the bill passed, Philadelphia, which eventually would add a thousand police to our force of six thousand with crime-bill funding, was graduating our first class of crime-bill-funded officers from our academy. I believe we were the first in the nation to do so. I had an idea. Since this was one of the president's best domestic achievements, we needed to keep it fresh in voters' minds. Wouldn't it be great to have their graduation ceremony in the Rose Garden, with the president of the United States to swear them in? The White House said "yes," and I rode the Metroliner down to Washington, accompanied by 222 uniformed, starry-eyed new Philadelphia police recruits. What a sight we were! The ceremony in the Rose Garden was even better. It was a perfect day. I presented the class to the president and Senator Biden, who was the prime sponsor of the bill. They both spoke eloquently. A great, great day!

As the president's reelection effort neared he, of course, called on me to raise money for the effort. Given all he had done for Philadelphia, I agreed to do so willingly, and we raised tons from Philadelphia businesspeople who understood what the president had done for us and wanted him to have four more years to do even more.

I will never forget one fund-raising visit the president made to Philadelphia. It was in the midst of all the heat he and the veep were receiving for some of the fund-raising excesses of the Democratic National Committee. He was scheduled to land at 4:00 P.M., go to a holding room to make phone calls, and then attend the fund-raiser at six and fly back at eight forty-five. The only reason for him coming to town was for the fund-raiser and I knew we were going to raise $1.5 million. With nothing else on the schedule, that was sure to be the story dominating the news the next day—not a good outcome. So when the president landed I asked him if he was hungry and he said, "Sure, I'm always hungry." (Me too!) So I detoured him to South Philly and Pat's Steaks—our famous cheesesteak stand where everyone in the Delaware Valley has eaten. The Secret Service wasn't too pleased, but they did their usual great job of protecting the president at our impromptu stop. We were accompanied by the terrific Philadelphia congress-man and party chairman Bob Brady. The president, Brady, and I ordered and, in the grand Philadelphia tradition, we ate them standing up. Brady taught the president the "Philadelphia lean"—it's the way you eat the cheesesteak leaning forward, so none of the sauce or other ingredients gets on your clothes. My idea turned out to be a master stroke. The next day our major newspaper, the *Inquirer*, had a big picture on the front page of President Clinton, Congressman Brady, and me leaning forward and eating cheese-steaks—a picture guaranteed to endear the president to every voter in the region. Oh, by the way, the story about the fund-raiser was buried on page nineteen. Boy, am I smart!

The president was a good fund-raiser not because he gave away government contracts or made deals—he didn't—but because he did the little things necessary to build loyalty among givers. There is no one I know in politics who does it better. He always remembers their names and birthdays, and he calls them to say hello periodically.

A perfect example of this occurred shortly after the president took office. He attended a fund-raiser for the Democratic National Committee at Lincoln Center in New York. The co-chairs of the event were my friend Bruce Ratner and one of my closest friends, Lew Katz. Lew is a great guy who has made a fortune and has given a good deal of it away to a host of good causes. He is also a very funny man with a unique sense of humor.

On this night it was decided that Bruce would introduce the president and Lew would introduce Bruce. But before they went onstage, Lew asked the president if while Bruce was speaking he, the president, would whisper something in Lew's ear; it didn't matter what it was. The president asked Lew why he wanted him to do it. Lew told him that while he was whispering something in his ear he, Lew, would be nodding and people would think he was giving advice to the president. Clinton shook his head with a mixture of wonder and disgust. When the time came, the president leaned over and whispered into Lew's ear, "Katz, you're a real putz!" Lew, always unflappable, kept a straight face and nodded yes several times. At the time Lew was in the parking business and there were many building owners in the audience at the fundraiser. Once they saw that Lew was so close to the president that he gave the president advice, almost every one of them gave Lew their parking concessions! Oh, my!

Of course, the biggest lapse in judgment the president made was Monica and his initial denial. No one, not even the staunchest

Clinton supporter, could defend his actions. But did his transgressions warrant impeachment? Were they the "high crimes and misdemeanors" that the framers of our Constitution had in mind when they drafted the impeachment clause? No way, no how. Not even close. The entire impeachment fiasco infuriated Democrats, and the American people punished the Republicans for it in the 1998 elections. I, along with many others, was infuriated by the clear hypocrisy of many of the president's most rabid Republican prosecutors.

The Philadelphia press hounded me for comments as impeachment neared, knowing my friendship with the president. Finally I decided to respond and held a press conference. I went out first and brought a tape by Jeannie C. Riley, the country singer whose big hit was "Harper Valley PTA." It was a song about a woman who was called on the carpet for wearing short skirts when she picked up her daughter from school. She went to the PTA meeting and responded by pointing out the moral failings of each PTA board member. The final verse ends with the famous line "You're all Harper Valley hypocrites." Well, I started out the press conference by playing the tape over my microphone. KYW radio, the market's number-one station, played the tape as a lead-in to their story.

Little did I know how prophetic this would turn out to be. Almost immediately and for more than another decade, Republicans who had denounced the president as "immoral" and who had been his most rigorous attackers were revealed to have moral transgressions as bad or worse than his. The list included:

- Newt Gingrich, Representative (R-GA): He led the charge on impeachment, and was later forced to admit having had an affair with an intern while married to his second wife.
- Henry Hyde, Representative (R-IL): He called the resolution to impeach a "reaffirmation of a set of values that are tarnished and dim these days, but it is given to us to restore them so our Founding Fathers would be proud." After the

hearings, Hyde admitted to having a four-year affair with a married mother of three after her husband accused him of ruining their marriage.

- John Ensign, Senator (R-NV): He called for the resignation of President Clinton in 1998. In 2009, he admitted to having had an affair with the wife of a close friend.
- Larry Craig, Senator (R-ID): He voted in the Senate to convict President Clinton. Did not run for reelection in 2008 because of a guilty plea of disorderly conduct following an arrest in a Minneapolis airport men's room on a charge of homosexual lewd conduct
- Steven C. LaTourette, Representative (R-OH): After voting for impeachment, it came to light that he was involved in a long-term affair with his chief of staff.
- Bob Barr, Representative (R-GA): After calling for impeachment, his wife signed a sworn affidavit that he cheated on her with Barr's soon-to-be third wife. He never refuted the claim.
- Robert Livingston, Representative (R-LA): He called for the impeachment of President Clinton, but resigned after the discovery of his own extramarital affairs.
- Dan Burton, Representative (R-IN): He famously said, "No [elected official] should be allowed to get away with these alleged sexual improprieties." He was later forced to admit that he had an affair that produced a child.
- Helen Chenoweth-Hage, Representative (R-ID): She aggressively called for President Clinton's impeachment and then admitted to her own affair with a married rancher.
- All "Harper Valley hypocrites!"

Well, President Clinton survived, and the distractions were great, but during the period of the impeachment he was amazing. He kept on plugging, kept on moving forward. He had an enviable capacity to shut things out, to not let the incredible flak he was taking slow him down. Some notable things President Clinton did during 1998 included: signing Ireland's Good Friday Peace Accords; issuing a directive prohibiting discrimination in federal employment based on sexual orientation; becoming the first president to visit China since Tienanmen Square; launching strikes against al-Qaeda targets; and signing the Class Size Reduction Initiative, the Charter School Expansion Act, and Head Start Expansion and Reauthorization. Not to mention getting a budget deal done. When asked how he managed to be so productive in the midst of all the controversy he said, "You just show up for work every day." When things got rough for me during my tenure as governor I would try to remember what he said, tune out all the BS, and keep fighting. In retrospect, it was amazing what his administration accomplished during this difficult time.

By the fall of 1999, with the 2000 presidential election looming, the Democratic National Committee was lagging far behind its Republican counterpart in fund-raising and was not doing an effective job of communicating how well the country was doing under the leadership of the Clinton-Gore administration. One day in mid-September, I was in Williamsburg, Virginia, at a meeting with Meryl Levitz and some of the city's tourism leaders and folks from Colonial Williamsburg, when I was told to call President Clinton. He asked me to come to the White House that night and, of course, I did.

When I got there, the president shocked the heck out of me by asking me to become chairman of the DNC. My main tasks would be to raise money and go on TV to deliver our message of peace and prosperity. I wasn't crazy about the idea—I was looking forward to resting in 2000 and preparing to run for governor—but you don't say no to the president.

In retrospect, I'm glad I did it. Though I had a number of highly publicized run-ins with the Gore consultants, I got to meet a lot of great people who cared very deeply about what happens in our country and who helped me mightily in my campaign for governor.

I will never forget something that occurred that night at the White House. While the president was pitching for me to take the job, we were interrupted by a call from Hillary, who was in New York campaigning for the Senate. We were in the president's living quarters, and he went to the next room to take the call. He left the door open and I could hear every word he said. He was on the phone for nearly half an hour. He was laughing and joking—I could tell that he and Hillary were swapping stories about New York politicians—and having a great time. I had always believed, and that call further convinced me, that Bill and Hillary have a deep, genuine love and sincere affection for each other. Notwithstanding their troubles, they have a strong love that is a whole lot more than just friendship.

After I left office as mayor in January 2000, I spent the next four months traveling the country doing fund-raisers with President Clinton. They were almost always fun, and it never ceased to amaze me how each time President Clinton spoke he would mesmerize the crowd and hold them in the palm of his hand. One night we were in Houston and, as was often the case, we had entertainment at the event. This night it was country singer Billy Ray Cyrus, not yet known as Miley's dad, and the great comedian Red Buttons. They were in the audience when the speaking program began. I spoke first and introduced the president. He spoke about where the country needed to go to meet the challenges of the new century and why Al Gore was the best person to lead us there. He was talking about meeting the challenge of providing health care, as Americans are living longer. He said that our life expectancy was extending and that if you lived to be sixty-five, now your average life expectancy had increased to eighty-three. As he spoke, as usual, you could hear a pin drop. But when he said "eighty-three," from the audience you could hear a loud, clear "Oy vey!" It was the eighty-three-year old Red Buttons. Later that night Red showed that at eighty-three, he was not ready to go. After the program, he went out with me and our DNC fund-raising staff—mostly women in their twenties and early thirties—and asked everyone for a date except me!

I had some very funny moments while on my four-month fund-raising circuit with President Clinton. We always ran late because he was never on time. I would always arrive at the event first, and part of my job was to keep the crowd from getting too anxious while waiting for the president. The DNC fund-raising staff and I would try to calm them by telling them the president was just five minutes away. Penny Lee, who did a great job leading our finance crew, and Michelle Singer, who always advanced the president, would always say that "the three biggest lies in the world were: I'll love you in the morning, the check is in the mail, and President Clinton is five minutes away."

One night we were scheduled to do two big-ticket fund-raising events in New York. The first was at Daniel's, a truly great restaurant. I met the president in a little back room. As was our custom, I briefed him about the makeup of the crowd. He then asked me to move him through both events quickly and not to let him eat anything because Hillary was cooking him dinner at home in Chappaqua.Talk about "mission impossible" times two! It was 7:00 P.M. and he was already half an hour behind schedule. I decided to switch the program so that he would speak at seven-fifteen, when everyone sat down to have dinner. The president is the world's greatest schmoozer and he genuinely loves to talk to people, so despite my best efforts, we didn't sit down until seven-forty. I was about to introduce the president when he noticed that the first course was lamb chops lollipops—one of his favorites. So he asked that we wait and he finally got up to speak at eight-fifteen. I told him to do a quick ten-to fifteen-minute speech and leave with no question-and-answer session. He finished talking at eight forty-five and then, unbelievably, opened it up for a Q&A. I tried to break in and pull him out three or four times, but he would have none of it. He answered a ton of questions, and not with a simple "yes" or "no." Needless to say, we left at nine-thirty.

We arrived at the famous Four Seasons restaurant at nine-fifty—a full hour and a half behind schedule. People were pissed. But, as he worked the crowd, one by one their anger faded. Bill Clinton made you feel like you were the most important person in the world when talking to you. We sat down to dinner at ten-thirty and all was well (except for his dinner date in Chappaqua). I had arranged for the president to speak before any food was served, but this time he noticed that the entrée was, yep—you guessed it—lamb chops. Again, we would wait until he had spoken. Well, you can guess the rest. He didn't start to speak until ten-fifty and after another Q&A and more totally futile attempts on my part to pull him, we left at eleven thirty-five. Good grief! Even with the presidential motorcade, they wouldn't have reached Chappaqua much before twelve-ten. Even if Hillary was a saint, although she often was, and still was awake, the president would have to eat every morsel she had cooked. I said a short prayer that lamb chops weren't on the menu!

CHAPTER 10

Animals I Have Known

I told you in the Introduction that politics was often wacky and sometimes very funny (though often it's funniest when it's not trying to be). When I first ran for office as a young thirty-two-year-old seeking to become district attorney, I had absolutely no idea of the role that animals—real and make-believe (mascots)—would play in my career. Donkeys (naturally), orangutans, parrots, hawks, pigs, and others have provided memorable moments in my career.

Let me start in 2000 with "Swifty, the Democratic Donkey." I was the chairman of the Democratic National Committee and one day Bridget Martin, who was our finance person in charge of labor, came to me extremely excited to tell me that Boilermakers' union members from Tennessee had agreed to donate a donkey to the DNC for use during the 2000 campaign. Bridget, who was bright and creative, thought that we could use the donkey as our mascot all across the country and that his tour would culminate in late August at our convention in Los Angeles. I have always loved animals, and mascots, too (as I will explain later), so I said "sure." Bridget was very excited and planned a debut for Swifty at a big Al Gore fund-raiser at the Tennessee Titans' football stadium in Nashville. I arrived outside the stadium about an hour before the event was to start and met Swifty, who was in a pen right next to the entrance that our guests were going to use to go inside. My first quick impression of Swifty was very good because he was a very noble, ruggedly handsome donkey, a great representative of our hardworking Democrats. But then I heard a thumping noise and looked more closely at Swifty, only to find, much to my dismay, that this was no ordinary donkey.

I was gripped by a growing sense of panic. If Swifty didn't calm down it could be a disaster. What would the press report? Would Swifty's unusual physical attributes take away from what was sure to be an incredible show of support from Al's hometown? I pulled myself together. After all, my success as mayor had convinced me that I was a great leader, an incredibly adept problem-solver, and that no crisis was too great for me. So I went inside the pen and talked calmly and soothingly to this most noble beast. My words and constant petting would surely calm Swifty's ardor. But no, it seemed to have the reverse effect, and although it didn't seem possible, the problem was soon scraping the bottom of the pen.

I had forgotten that our fifty state party chairmen were in Nashville and were arriving half an hour early. They began walking in and as they passed Swifty (there was a big sign announcing him as Swifty, the Democratic Donkey, the official DNC mascot), the male chairmen snickered and their women counterparts reacted with shock and disgust, a budding disaster. Only the female chair from Pennsylvania seemed amused and actually posed for a picture with Swifty, a fact that filled me with pride for my home state.

Well, Swifty's debut was a flat-out disaster, but a good leader knows how to do damage control. So when I reached Washington the next day I told Bridget to politely inform the boilermakers that we were returning the randy beast to them. Half an hour later, she came into my office and said that when she told Swifty's owner about the problem he offered to "lop it off." Oh, good—the thought of PETA tormenting us right to Election Day was almost too much for me to bear. So Swifty the five-legged donkey, in all his glory, stayed on as the DNC mascot.

I was daunted, but not defeated. I took decisive action. Swifty's tour was dramatically curtailed, and I ordered him fitted with a blanket that literally reached the ground. Swifty's enormity would be a DNC secret, though I realized people might think it a little odd that he was wearing a blanket in June, July, and August. Clearly, though, that was better than shocking America.

I decided that I needed to see Swifty clad in his blanket. I felt a little bit like Ike reviewing the troops when I went to visit him at a college rally. At first I thought that the blanket, which had the DNC logo on its side, looked good and had solved the problem. But when I walked behind Swifty, my heart sank. The blanket only covered his sides! I gave up, but immediately canceled Swifty's trip to the convention, where we had planned to put him outside with hundreds of other exhibits. But Bridget told me that the boilermakers, and perhaps all of the building trades, would be offended by this.

I was at my wits' end. Surely the national press, particularly Fox News, would discover Swifty and embarrass us big-time, but when I saw the layout of the exhibits I knew what I had to do. I exiled our DNC mascot to the exhibit site farthest away from the Staples Center, nearly a mile away. When we arrived in LA, I was racked with guilt, so my chief of staff, David Yarkin, and I went to visit Swifty. By now he had come to recognize me, and as we came close the thumping increased in volume and rapidity. My guilt vanished and our exile worked. We had our mascot for nearly six months and not a hint of scandal. Of course, in retrospect, there was no way for a reporter to report on our embarrassment without embarrassing their own institution, which they seem to do more now every day.

While writing this book, I looked into bringing Swifty the five-legged donkey out to bookstores with me. If you see me somewhere without him, you'll know that publishers are a timid bunch of wusses, too.

During my tenure as mayor, I did a commercial with an orangutan, an actor named Bailey. The ad was for the reopening of the Mammal House at the Philadelphia Zoo. It was important because the zoo's Primate House had been destroyed by a tragic fire on Christmas Eve 1995, killing most of the primates. There had been no replacement for nearly two years, but it was finally reopening. The theme of the ad was that Bailey was trying to find his way to the zoo for the opening, and as mayor I had a map and was showing him how to get there. Each time I gave him direction to take a specific street Bailey would nod, as if he understood me. While we were doing the commercial I became convinced that Bailey was smarter than a great deal of the elected officials I had worked with. After we were done filming, Bailey reached over and planted a wet kiss on my cheek. I decided he was a lot nicer, too.

As a general rule, a politician should never pose with an animal, unless it is trained as an actor like Bailey. I violated that rule to pose with a hawk that had been nurtured back to health by the Schuylkill Valley Nature Center, a great environmental organization and venue. My good friend Dave Montgomery, the principal owner of the Phillies, had been chair of their board, and when he asked I couldn't say no. They had told me there was no chance the hawk could turn on me, but when they put his claws on my arm and told me to lift him into the air I wasn't so sure. The hawk looked fierce and not too happy, but he was anxious to get into the wild and, as it turned out, had very little interest in me.

My career has also involved escapades with animal mascots. The Delaware River separates Philadelphia and South Jersey, and there used to be a ferry that took people back and forth. When I was mayor we decided to bring it back, especially since a great amphitheater had opened up on the Jersey side and was booking big-name acts. We believed that young people from the Philly side would love to take the ferry over rather than fight the traffic (we were right). Well, we decided to debut the ferry with a flourish. I was going to take the first ride over, and the governor of New Jersey, Jim Florio, was going to meet us when we docked.

Now, Jim Florio may well be the best and most honorable elected official I have ever met, but he has absolutely no sense of humor. I mean none. But I had more than enough whimsy and mischievousness for both of us.

So I decided I would take along a few fellow passengers, but they would all be mascots: the Villanova Wildcat, the St. Joseph's Hawk, the Textile Ram, the Drexel Dragon, Swoop the Philadelphia Eagle, the Phillie Phanatic, and many, many more.

So the ferry was loaded with me and twenty-four mascots—no one else. As we drew near the dock, I caught sight of Governor Florio. He had a slight frown on his face. As we drew closer, his frown grew bigger and bigger and he had a look of total amazement as he glanced at the ferry inhabited by one mayor and two dozen mascots. It was clear that he was thinking, "Rendell is totally nuts!" There is probably a lot of truth in that thought.

Though many animals amuse use and are a source of fun, some— those great animal athletes—can lift us and inspire us. You can think of many examples—from the great Secretariat, who captivated the country, to the many courageous police dogs who give their lives to protect us. During the spring of 2005 a little red horse captured the imagination of the Philadelphia region, the state, and even the entire nation, especially the children who fell in love with his name, Smarty Jones.

Smarty was an unlikely Triple Crown contender. He was smallish, didn't have royal bloodlines, and didn't train in the bluegrass of Kentucky, but rather at the decidedly pedestrian Philadelphia Park in Bucks County. His owner wasn't one of racing's first families, but was a Philadelphia car dealer. But Smarty roared into the Kentucky Derby undefeated. Not only had he never been beaten, but also he had never been passed. He wasn't the favorite, but he won the Derby going away. Smarty's love affair with Greater Philadelphia was on. It spiraled into a tsunami of affection for "Little Red."

I love Triple Crown racing, and as a crafty politician who was up for reelection the next year, I decided to climb on the Smarty bandwagon and went to visit him at Philadelphia Park. I was escorted to his stall by John Servis, his great trainer. Contrary to the conventional wisdom, Smarty was asleep not standing up, but on his stomach. When I came in, John exhorted Smarty to get up and meet the governor. Smarty was unmoved. But then four TV crews arrived, and when they entered the stable Smarty bolted upright and started preening.

Notwithstanding the cold shoulder he gave me, I became a rabid Smarty fan. When I got an invitation from Smarty's owner, Roy Chapman, for Midge and me to sit with them at the Preakness, we accepted. We were there when Smarty blew the field away, winning by a Preakness record 10½ lengths. As Smarty pulled away and went farther and farther ahead, it was breathtaking. After the race Roy wanted us to come down to the winner's circle with him. We did and were on the platform where Roy was presented the trophy by Maryland governor Bob Ehrlich. After the ceremony, Roy, who was confined to a wheelchair because of respiratory problems, was wheeled down past us. As he went by me he grabbed my arm and said, "Governor, how about some of the state's truck business?" Once a car dealer, always a car dealer!

After the Preakness victory, Philadelphia went wild. The city and the region had not had a winner since the 1982 Philadelphia 76ers—nearly two and a half decades earlier. People believed Smarty couldn't possibly lose the Belmont. Everywhere I went people asked me if we were going to have a parade. I thought everyone had gone mad. Can you imagine this incredibly valuable horse being drawn on a flatbed truck down Broad Street or actually loafing down 4½ miles of concrete city streets? Good grief!

But once again, sports broke the city's heart and the nation's, too. When Smarty was trucked from Philadelphia to Belmont Park people lined the streets to cheer him on. He was truly the people's choice. On race day I and tens of thousands of Philadelphians were up at Belmont Park. Enthusiasm was incredibly high, only dampened for a minute when total silence fell upon hearing of the passing of President Reagan. When the race started Smarty shot out to the lead, but was buffeted and challenged by one horse after another. At the top of the stretch he was four lengths ahead, but he ran out of gas, and seventy-five yards from the finish he was passed for the first time in his life, by Birdstone. When the race ended, the record-breaking crowd, which seemed earlier to have produced a deafening crescendo of sound, fell totally silent. Birdstone's trainer almost apologized for winning. More than a hundred thousand people shared communal grief.

Schoolchildren all over the country were crushed, and Smarty received thousands of letters from kids saying how sorry they were that he lost. Kids, being kids, will get over Smarty's loss—I never will!!

CHAPTER 11

How to Get Uninvited to a Christmas Party You Were Never Invited To

Al Gore is a funny guy. He has a great personality. He has a good heart and would have made a fine president.

Al Gore is a funny guy? He has a great personality? Am I crazy?

Yes, yes, and yes. I have always maintained that I'm a little crazy—you have to be to have spent more than three decades in my business. But the real Al Gore—the one the public never saw, the one his consultants never let the public see, is a funny, personable, warm, and extremely nice man.

Case in point: it was late September 2000, and I was the chairman of the Democratic National Committee. The vice president and I were in New Orleans for an important fund-raiser and rally. Louisiana was still in play; the polls showed we had a chance to carry it. Two days before, after the first Gore-Bush debate, I was in the spin room and was approached by Mary McGrory, a nationally renowned reporter. Mary was one of my idols. As a kid growing up in New York City I read the *New York Post*. It was then a quality newspaper with progressive leanings and with great writers and columnists such as Murray Kempton and Mary McGrory. So when Mary asked me, "Should the Gore campaign be using President Clinton more?" I couldn't give her the official Gore campaign spin. I, as is my basic instinct, told the truth and said "yes." Of course, we should have let President Clinton campaign in key states such as Pennsylvania, Ohio, Missouri, West Virginia, Arkansas, and Michigan. His approval ratings were very high, and no one, including Al Gore, made the case for electing Al Gore any better than Bill Clinton did. The Gore consultants (who blew the election for Al) thought that Clinton would turn off undecided voters who didn't like him or who cared about values issues, and they decided to ostracize him from the campaign. Great strategy! Great idea! If we don't use Bill Clinton, people will forget that Al Gore was the vice president in the administrations of "what's-his-name." How can smart people be so dumb? Easy answer: These inside-the-Beltway consultants always, I mean always, underestimate the intelligence of the American people.

Well, back to that night in New Orleans. My comments to Mary McGrory caused an uproar (it seemed like I was always causing an uproar in 2000). The headline of the next morning's *USA Today* was "Top Democrats Call for Clinton on Campaign Trail." The story went on to quote six or seven "top Democrats" but, of course, only one was named. The others were identified as simply "a top Democrat" or a "Democratic source." Oh, boy! As soon as I read the article I knew there was trouble ahead.

Right before the fund-raising jazz concert I was told by my DNC aide, Michelle Singer, that the vice president wanted to see me. I could tell by the look on her face that this was not a social call. I was ushered into a small room backstage and Al was there alone. For the next twenty minutes he ripped me a new rear end. I had created an unnecessary controversy that had taken attention away from the campaign's message. Never one to grin and bear it, I took one last shot at trying to convince him to use the president. After being ripped for another ten minutes, I fought back. "Al," I said, "everyone knows you were Bill Clinton's vice president. And everyone knows you're not Bill Clinton, but you guys have had an extremely successful eight years. The country is in great shape. Let's remind the people of that. And besides, every elected official I talk to begs me to let the president campaign in their state." He rebuffed me. The Beltway consultants had convinced him that all state and local politicians are either corrupt or stupid and, in truth, some of us are. But by no means all of us. And we know a whole lot more about what our constituents are thinking and what moves them than does any pollster or consultant.

And on that steamy night in New Orleans, I believe the election was lost and the course of world history changed. I have no doubt that if we had used President Clinton we would have carried Arkansas, New Hampshire, Ohio, Missouri, and West Virginia. In fact, I spent an entire day campaigning in West Virginia a week before the election, and at the airport that night, a few of the state's leading Democratic politicians cornered me in a private room. They asked if the vice president would be coming back to West Virginia in the last week. I said "no," and they said "good." (A coal state such as West Virginia was very cool to Al's environmental initiatives.) Then they asked if they could have President Clinton for a day. I said, "Guys, I've gotten in big trouble for saying we should use Clinton more, but I believe he would be best used in states with large minority populations to increase turnout." They responded, "Mayor, no offense, but you don't understand. West Virginia is a hillbilly state and Bill Clinton is a hillbilly!" Ah, the beauty of Bill Clinton—a down-home hillbilly to West Virginians and Tennesseans and Arkansans and a brilliant, urbane sophisticate to New Yorkers and Californians!

I said that Al Gore is among other things a very decent and nice man, and he truly is. After ripping me in the back room for thirty minutes, we went out to listen to the jazz concert. He and I were sitting on either side of Tipper and, as the concert went on, he leaned across her to tell me something about each performer. Al knew I didn't care very much about jazz, but it was his way of saying, "Hey, I know how hard you have worked for me the last ten months without a day off, going from city to city, and I forgive you for screwing up." He couldn't say it to me directly, but what he did meant the world to me. Yes, Al Gore is a very nice man and the most knowledgeable man I have ever met. He knows virtually everything about government and the issues it faces.

A perfect example of this could have been seen at any of the countless fund-raisers for the DNC I attended with the vice president. Because of the fund-raising scandals of 1996 (such as the Buddhist monks who took vows of poverty giving the DNC $5,000 each), the DNC had adopted a rule that our fund-raising events were open to the press. The Republicans, who have absolutely no shame when it comes to fund-raising, kept theirs closed.

This meant that the press could come in, take pictures, and stay to hear my introduction of the veep and his speech. Al's consultants had convinced him that the only way he could lose the 2000 election was by making a mistake, so his basic presentation in front of the reporters and contributors was 100 percent pabulum-safe as could be, American as apple pie, and delivered in a veritable wooden trance.

When the reporters left, I would try to persuade Al to do a question-and-answer session, in an almost desperate attempt to convince people that they had not just given $10,000 to a complete zombie. Most times Al was willing, and during Q&A, with no reporters present and no fear of making a mistake, he was warm, engaging, funny, and incredibly smart. If America had seen that Al Gore the election would have been a landslide and we never would have learned about "hanging chads."

We went all over the country, and no one—and I mean no one—ever asked him a question he couldn't answer. I will never forget a fund-raising lunch we had in Washington, DC. Twelve people paid $50,000 each to have an intimate lunch with the VP and me ($1 for me, $49,999 for Al). After lunch, we had a Q&A where a lady asked, "Mr. Vice President, how do you think the federal government should respond to the challenge brought about by the advent of GMOs?"

A chill went up my spine. Someone had finally asked Al a question he couldn't answer. (At the time this was, essentially, a question about European agricultural import policies and, while environmental, not an issue commonly put in a president's portfolio to manage.) Wrong again! Without missing a beat, Al gave a five-minute dissertation on how we should manage and control the use of "genetically modified organisms." Wow!

My tenure as DNC chairman was a stormy one almost from the beginning.

Potential Republican candidate George W. Bush had been ambushed by a *Boston Globe* reporter who asked him to name the leaders of some fairly obscure Asian nations. Needless to say, he couldn't get even one right, and it caused a furor. I was appearing on the cable TV show *Crossfire* that evening with RNC chair Jim Nicholson. The host, Paul Begala, opened the show by showing a tape of Bush failing to answer any of the questions correctly. Then he turned to Nicholson and asked, "Does this shocking lack of knowledge about world leaders disqualify George Bush from being a viable candidate for president?" Jim hemmed and hawed but did not do a very good job sticking up for Bush. Then Begala asked me the same question and I replied, "Absolutely not. Paul, I think it was a cheap shot by the reporter. I'm not concerned that Governor Bush didn't know the names of those foreign leaders. He can get that from a briefing book. I would have been more impressed if the reporter asked the governor, 'How could a Republican president ask India and Pakistan to give up their nuclear weapons when the party is against the nuclear test ban treaty?'"

Well, there it was. The chairman of the DNC did a better job defending Bush than his RNC counterpart. It caused a firestorm. Begala, a liberal Democrat, was outraged that I had defended Bush. Back at DNC headquarters virtually everyone was saying I should be fired. The tempers raged for two days until the press spoke with President Clinton, who had been in Europe, as he was boarding *Air Force One*. He gave almost the same answer as I did, saying that Bush had plenty of time to learn those names. So from that moment on, I just kept telling people, "If you have any problems with what I said, take it up with the big guy!"

Why did I do it? Why did I defend Bush? Because what I said was the truth, and I have always tried to answer questions truthfully, to say what I believe, and never to BS people. I believe that it builds my credibility as a fair person, not a partisan attack dog. So when I did criticize the other side, and I knew throughout the long campaign of 2000 that I would often do so, I would be listened to. I knew that was the right approach, but a few months later, in early July, I was in the Montgomery, Alabama, airport when a man came up to me. He looked at me and asked, "Are you that Democrat guy on TV?" I replied "yes" and then he said, "Thanks for not yelling at us. Thanks for not demonizing the other guys." As the election year went on, I heard that over and over again. Real people who are undecided in almost every election do not want to be yelled at. They do not believe that we are always right and the other party is always wrong. They want to hear facts and well-reasoned arguments, but they rarely do. That is why I believe that I built up a bit of credibility with these voters and was very effective in my role as party spokesman, despite incurring the wrath of our party's zealots on more than one occasion.

But with my usual perfect timing, I saved the best for last. I had anticipated leaving my DNC position a week after the November election. But the Florida incident happened and the election went on and on and on. The recount became mired in tales of hanging chads and older Jewish voters in Fort Lauderdale voting for Pat Buchanan. As we all know, the case wound up in the US Supreme Court to determine whether the Florida Supreme Court had correctly ordered a statewide recount. The Court heard arguments on the case on December 12, and the entire nation watched anxiously for the decision. As luck would have it, I was booked on Chris Matthews *Hardball* program the night of December 18.

We were talking about the case and its legality, and trying to anticipate what the Court would do. (I had thought that the conservative-majority Court would let the state court's decision stand and that that the recount would proceed; so much for my legal acumen.) But at ten o'clock that night word reached us that the Supreme Court had decided the case and overruled the Florida Supreme Court and banned the recount. I disagreed violently with the decision. I thought that the Court had abandoned its states' rights precedents and given the election to George W. Bush based solely on partisan politics. It was brutally disheartening, but it was also clear to me that it was over.

Chris Matthews then asked me the fatal question, "What do you think Al Gore should do now?" I should have said, "Well, that is up to him and his campaign team and I'm sure they will review the Court ruling and make a decision shortly." But oh, no, not me! I had to tell the whole truth, nothing but the truth. I couldn't give the Gores any time to even grieve. I said, "I believe Al Gore should and will do the right thing—concede the election and make a great speech tomorrow, which will unify the country." Less than twenty-four hours later, Al Gore conceded and made a great speech that unified the nation. But notwithstanding this, when I gave my answer shortly after 10:00 P.M., all hell broke loose.

Within minutes, other DNC officials and the Gore campaign disavowed my comments, ripped me, and all but called me a treasonous traitor. As I sat on the seat at Video Link—a studio in Philadelphia—call after call came in asking me how I could have said that. Chris Matthews, of course, picked up on the controversy and kept me on the air for another hour, answering their charges. It was agony and I don't think I have ever felt so nervous or so afraid. I saw my whole political career flashing in front of my eyes. In fact, the next day, the *Philadelphia Inquirer* wrote that I had done irreparable damage to my chances of being elected governor.

But an amazing thing happened in the next few days. Everywhere I went people would stop their cars and yell at me, "Hang in there! You did the right thing!" or "You told the truth, you're the best!" In fact, my statement turned out to be a plus, adding to my reputation as a blunt, honest guy who speaks the truth and tells what is on his mind.

There was one humorous thing that happened during that fateful night. At about one-fifteen my wife, Midge, was awakened by a call to our home from an aide to Tipper Gore, who announced that our invitation to the Gores' Christmas party was being withdrawn. There was only one problem with that: we had never been invited!

CHAPTER 12

How My Love Affair with Philadelphia Made Me Governor

My time as DNC chairman was ending. I had promised the president that I would stay on through the election, though the recount in Florida extended my time. A new chair was to be elected and began serving on February 1, 2001.

On the Tuesday of his last week in office, I received a call from the president asking me to assemble, at five o'clock that afternoon, the DNC staff then serving and anyone who had worked for the DNC during his presidency, so he could thank them.

A tall order, but we got almost everyone there, and on a very cold January night more than 200 staffers crammed into a room that had a fire department capacity of 125 and turned it into a veritable sauna. I introduced the president and he began to speak. The previously rambunctious young staffers grew silent and, as always, you could have heard the proverbial pin drop. The president began by telling those great young people that there must have been times during their work at the DNC when their friends, and even their families, asked them why they did it—why they worked terribly long hours for very little pay and in horrible working conditions and why they wasted their time working in such a dirty, rotten business such as politics, which was so bitterly partisan and so rancorous.

He went on to say, "When they ask you why, tell them you did it to help 23.5 million people find jobs; that you did it to help more African Americans and Latinos climb out of poverty than at any other time in our nation's history; that you did it to help 4 million young people who never believed that they had a chance to go to college to get an education through the Hope Scholarship program; that you worked for so little pay to help protect the environment and natural beauty that the Lord had given America; and that you endured the terrible working conditions to save a million Muslim Kosovars from genocide at the hands of the butcher Milosevic. Because that's exactly what you did, by helping to elect Al Gore and myself. That's why you endured the long hours, the low pay, and all the grief from others."

When he finished there wasn't a dry eye in the house, including mine. Bill Clinton had just validated what these young people had done with their lives and explained more clearly than anyone else ever could have why, in retrospect, despite all the frustrations and disappointments, I wouldn't trade the thirty-three years I spent in government and politics for anything—I mean *anything*—in the world. We had had the chance to change people's lives, to create opportunity for people who had none, and to protect people who cannot make it alone. How can you put a price tag on that? You can't!

Sometime around then, I was having lunch with David Cohen. I was laying out for him my plans to run for governor and my strategy for the campaign. David, always more cautious than I am (which usually was a good thing), was skeptical that I could win—with good reason. No Philadelphian had been elected governor in nearly a century. Besides that daunting fact, if I decided to run I would be opposing Bob Casey Jr., the son of a former governor of the same name. Bob Jr. was the state auditor general and had been reelected in 2000 by a margin of more than a million votes.

David was concerned that a thumping defeat in the primary for governor would somehow detract from the legacy he and I had established during my tenure as mayor. I wasn't! First, I didn't believe that a loss would tarnish what we accomplished while I was mayor. I believed that if that did happen, people would just chalk it up to the anti-Philadelphia bias in the state and it would not reflect on my time as mayor. Second, I don't give a hoot about my legacy. I didn't then and I don't now.

One of my great assets as a leader has been my understanding that I am not the smartest guy in the room. This is often a failing of many mayors, governors, and presidents, but I knew that David was far smarter than I am. But I also knew that this time he was wrong because I knew something he didn't. I knew from the constant contact I had with people from the Philadelphia region that their affection for me was incredibly strong and that their desire to have a governor from this part of the state was equally strong. That feeling would be crucial if we were to change the traditional voting pattern in the Democratic primaries for governor. You see, the Philadelphia region always turned out less than its registration, compared to the rest of the state. So, for example, if our five-county region had 40 percent of the registered Democrats in the state, it would traditionally cast about 31 percent of the total primary vote. I was sure that wouldn't be the case with me on the ballot. I was certain there would be a strong desire to vote for the hometown guy.

Well, despite all the naysayers and all the experts who said I couldn't win, I decided to run. I spent the rest of 2001 traveling the state and kicked off the official campaign in early January. It didn't start out very well. The first poll had Casey up by 25 points, and he received the endorsement of the Democratic State Committee. So I was running against the organization again,

I was the outsider once more. Even in Philadelphia fifty out of sixty-seven ward leaders were for Casey—hard to believe!

I had another hunch, though. I thought we could switch a lot of southeastern Republicans and independents to register as Democrats. In Pennsylvania we have a closed primary system—you can only vote in the Democratic primary if you are registered as a Democrat. Again, David and Neil Oxman, our brilliant media consultant, thought I was crazy. But I knew that we had an ace in the hole above and beyond the hometown support, and it was the abortion issue. The only Republican candidate, Attorney General Mike Fisher, was prolife, as was Bob Casey. With President Bush in the White House prochoice voters were worried that *Roe v. Wade* would be overturned and that the legality of abortion would be left up to the states. It was well known that if *Roe* fell, the Pennsylvania legislature would pass a bill making abortion criminal, and only a veto by the governor could stop it from becoming law. I prevailed and we invested significant resources in an effort to change registrations. We mailed people a letter asking them to switch and enclosed a registration form for them to do so by mail. We promised that after the primary, win or lose, we would send them another form so they could switch back. We phone-banked to the people who received the letters, again asking them to switch.

My hunch was rewarded. Was it ever! We switched more than fifty thousand Republicans and independents statewide. Most of those came from Philadelphia and its suburbs. The switchers were motivated by their desire to vote for me (many suburbanites told me that they had been waiting for twenty-five years for the chance to vote for me in a primary) and in part because of the abortion issue. We didn't switch all of my fans, however. I received a letter and a very nice contribution from an eighty-five-year old lifelong Republican who said he wanted to switch so he could vote for me but didn't because he was worried he would die before he could switch back and he didn't want to die as a Democrat! He probably believed that all Democrats go directly to hell.

Well, the campaign rolled on. I was a relentless campaigner. I went all over the state campaigning in every single county. Local newspapers noted that I had visited their small county five times and Casey had yet to campaign there. We were narrowing the gap each day, and we received the endorsements of almost every newspaper in the state. With seven days left I came home and would spend the rest of the campaign in southeastern Pennsylvania, driving turnout. As Election Day approached, enthusiasm kept building. On Election Day I went all around the city and suburbs visiting polling places. Turnout was high everywhere, and I was pumped! At 6:00 P.M. we were in Delaware County and decided to go back downtown. As the bus drove through the county and through West Philadelphia, I saw volunteers on almost every street corner wearing blue "Rendell for Governor" T-shirts. When we got to downtown the streets were a collage of blue people and signs. It brought tears to my eyes. Whether I was going to win or lose I would find out in a few more hours, but I knew then that I had forged a special relationship with the people of my extended hometown. That relationship has never changed. My wife has always said that in a place that is as tough as can be toward its heroes—athletes, news anchors, politicians—my biggest accomplishment is to have maintained such a high level of popularity for thirty-three years. I would learn that for sure a couple of hours later.

The polls closed at eight o'clock. I knew I had won by eight-thirty. We had volunteers at polling places throughout Philadelphia and the four suburban counties. As soon as the polls closed and the vote was totaled, they called in the returns. The turnout was astounding for a primary election, and the margins were even more amazing. I won precincts by 197 to 9; 311 to 24; 208 to 16; 381 to 44—and they weren't aberrations. When all the votes were in I won with a 56 percent to 44 percent margin despite carrying only 11 of the 67 counties. The fundamental belief that persuaded me to run when nobody thought I could win was borne out big-time. The Philadelphia region had 40 percent of the registered Democrats in the state but cast nearly 45 percent of the total primary vote. In the previous five governors' primaries the region had averaged only about 34 percent. The general election was more of the same. I won by 9 percentage points despite winning only 18 of the 67 counties.

My love affair with my extended hometown continued through my last election—my reelection in 2006. As hard as it was to believe, my margin of victory in the 5 Philadelphia counties actually increased. Statewide I carried 34 counties and won by more than 20 percentage points—and many of those counties were traditionally Republican. But the Philadelphia region results were breathtaking: in Philadelphia I received nearly 90 percent of the vote (383,339 to 45,502); in the four counties: Bucks—70 percent; Delaware—74 percent; Montgomery—72 percent; and Chester—65 percent. All of the suburban counties except Montgomery have significant Republican registration edges. What a great way to end my electoral career. What a great feeling! It made all the frustration and disappointment worthwhile. It made all the controversy, partisanship, and bickering seem irrelevant. It was a resounding vote of confidence by the people who know me best.

CHAPTER 13

Lobbyists' Rule

No Money for School

Most Americans still believe what Abe Lincoln said about our democracy—that it's "of the people, by the people, for the people." Sadly, if that ever was the case, it sure isn't today. We are now a government of the rich and powerful, by the lobbyists and for the special interests. This is true in Washington, DC, in Albany, in Sacramento, in Springfield, in Harrisburg, in Tallahassee, and in each and every one of our other state capitals.

A few examples: There is nothing more democratic, nothing more "for the people," then an increase in the minimum wage. In 2007 the federal minimum wage was $5.15, and Senator Kennedy had drafted a bill to raise it to $7.25. That may not seem like much, but when you are making $10,500 a year, a $4,200 raise is like manna from heaven. This legislation should have been easy to pass. Who could be against it? Well, for starters, President

Bush and much of the congressional Republican leadership. They claimed it would hurt business.

Senator Kennedy persevered, as only he could, and basically shamed Congress into passing it into law. But while they were at it, Republicans (and some Democrats) in Congress prepared some 150 amendments to provide more than $240 billion in tax breaks that were nothing more than giveaways to the special interests. At the end of the day, to pass the minimum-wage increase the Democrats had to accept $8.3 billion in tax breaks for businesses. Clearly Washington lobbyists for big business got what they wanted out of that bill. In spite of a booming economy, businesses walked away with new IRS rules that permitted them to write off improvements to retail and other leased space more quickly and a special giveaway permitting small businesses to write off the first $112,000 in capital investment quickly rather than amortize the investment over the life of the capital asset. Both of these tax breaks shield profits from taxation. The only way proponents of raising the minimum wage to help those people who earn it could get it passed into law would be by voting for all these special-interest giveaways.

Another example of the power of lobbyists and special interests is the clout wielded by the National Rifle Association. The NRA can and has defeated any attempt in Pennsylvania to impose common-sense limitations on the sale or distribution of firearms. This is true in most states and in Washington, DC, too.

As governor I tried to get legislation passed that would limit a person to buying only one handgun a month. This would have significantly limited what is called "straw purchasing," which occurs when a lawful buyer (no criminal record, no history of mental problems) buys ten handguns, all the same make, all automatic pistols, at one time. He or she waits for a week or so, then goes into high-crime areas of a city and sells them to people who cannot legally buy them in a store (convicted felons, people with mental problems, juveniles). This person will often sell them for two, three, or four times what was paid for them. In most urban areas nearly 40 percent of all guns used in crimes were purchased legally, but used to commit a crime by someone else, usually a felon or a juvenile.

My proposed legislation would still allow an individual to buy twelve handguns a year (a married couple could buy twenty-four between them). Who could possibly need more than that? Who could possibly oppose it when police officers and kids in Philadelphia are being shot? The NRA and the lobbyists did. They said they feared it was a "slippery slope." To show you the absolute absurdity of their position, I debated a representative of gun manufacturers on this issue, and the best he could come up with was to ask me what a business owner would do if he wanted to buy his employees a handgun for Christmas. I couldn't resist. I replied, "Leaving aside the horrific thought of someone celebrating the birthday of Jesus Christ by giving a gift of a gun, you can always buy gift certificates in each employee's name—one gun a month." Notwithstanding my debating skills, the NRA killed the bill in committee. It never even got to a vote.

The best example of the power of the lobbyists and their employers, the special interests, is what happens to legislation that has no special-interest support, that has no lobbyists to beat the drum for it. Public education falls into that category. One of my primary goals when I went to Harrisburg was to improve our K–12 public school system and to reduce the huge difference in education spending between the wealthier and the poorer districts. As I have already detailed, when I was governor we increased education spending by more than $4 billion annually, and the improvement in student achievement was dramatic—the best of any state in the country. But it didn't happen without a fight, without horrible bloodletting. In each of my eight years as governor I battled with the legislature over education funding, and in three years—2003, 2009, and 2010—we didn't get budgets approved until December 20, October 9, and July 6, respectively. We were supposed to have a budget by July 1.

In 2003, my first year, I proposed a $500 million increase in education funding for early childhood programs such as pre-kindergarten and full-day kindergarten. The legislature balked, but my resolve never wavered from the day I proposed the increase in my budget address. The next day I toured the state by plane, pushing my education budget. I was pleased to find a great deal of support from parents and, of course, educators, but I was taken by something that occurred at my last stop, at Norristown High School, in a large, poor urban district. I was introduced by Paul Perry, the senior class president, and in his introduction he asked, "Governor, can you tell us why in Montgomery County, one of the richest counties in America, some children are given PalmPilots to begin the school year and here, some children aren't given books?" Listening to him, I felt ashamed. Not as governor—I had only been governor for about seven weeks—but I felt ashamed as an adult Pennsylvanian and as a parent who could afford to send his son to a Montessori school when he was three and four years old and to Penn Charter, the best private school in the state, from kindergarten through twelfth grade. (In one of those great moments that sometimes happen in public service, six years later I told that story to a "Teach for America" conference and, unbeknownst to me, Paul was in the audience as a newly minted teacher.)

The budget deadlock lasted for the next nine months. We finally compromised and won nearly $300 million of additional funding, and in all our achievement gains none were as startling as those in early childhood. But the nine-month battle was tortuous, I was new as governor, and it was extremely frustrating. At a press conference one day in October I was asked about the impasse and I replied, "The trouble with this building is that it's run by lobbyists. They almost always get what they want. The problem with education funding is that the schoolchildren of Pennsylvania don't have any lobbyists. I'll stand up for them and fight for them every single day that I'm governor."

The battle for adequate education funding lasted for all eight years that I was governor. My insistence that it be increased every year until every single district was funded at adequate levels was opposed by Republican legislators whose sole goal was to reduce spending. This caused us to reach impasses, and every year we failed to get a budget on time. I didn't care. I was bound and determined to give every child in the commonwealth the chance to reach their full potential. That was far more important than "getting a budget done on time." Our intransigence paid off—we increased funding every year, even in 2009 and 2010, in the midst of the recession, and we were the only state to do so. I'm glad we stood up and fought for our kids. Let the record show that they are much better off because of it, and so is the commonwealth of Pennsylvania!

CHAPTER 14

"Behold the Turtle"

I t was 11:00 P.M. on the evening of November 7, 2006, and I was standing on the stage at the Warwick Hotel looking out over a packed, sweaty ballroom. They were wildly celebrating the fact that I had just been reelected as governor of Pennsylvania by more than 20 points, garnering more than 60 percent of the vote. A little more than three years earlier I had raised taxes by $2.7 billion, the second-largest increase in the state's history. My opponent, Lynn Swann, had raised more than $14 million and put almost all of it on TV, attacking me for doing so. My mind drifted back to early February of that same year when I was at the Super Bowl in Detroit watching the Pittsburgh Steelers battle the Seattle Seahawks. They were honoring all prior Super Bowl MVPs, a group Lynn Swann belonged to, and they ran out on the field one at a time. When Lynn came out, more than forty thousand

Pittsburghers roared their approval. A few days later the first poll came out and we were dead even.

But here we were just nine months later and we had won a crushing landslide victory. I started my victory speech without the usual thank yous—I did that later—because I had a very important message I wanted to deliver:

> Today Pennsylvania voted overwhelmingly for a government that is willing to invest in creating opportunities for its citizens through education and growth. Today Pennsylvanians overwhelmingly voted for a government that is willing to look to the future and invest in cutting-edge technologies and new sources of clean, homegrown energy. And today Pennsylvanians voted overwhelmingly for a government that cares deeply about the people it represents and is willing to invest in whatever is necessary to protect its most vulnerable citizens. That is exactly the type of government I pledge to give the people of Pennsylvania for the next four years.

How did this happen? To understand, you have to know the context of the four years that preceded that night. I was sworn in as governor on January 21, 2003. On that day, I was handed a proposed budget for fiscal year 2004 (beginning on July 1, 2003) by the outgoing Republican governor, Mark Schweiker, that had a $2.4 billion deficit. The state was facing a continuing revenue shortfall as the result of a significant recession. I had five weeks to prepare our budget and present it to the legislature. I had campaigned honestly when confronted with the question of what I would do to deal with our deficit. Although I was certain we could drastically reduce the cost of operating state government as I had done in Philadelphia, that effort would take some time, and it was likely we would need to raise taxes. I won handily because the voters were realistic about our situation.

In addition to bridging the $2.4 billion gap, I had said I wanted to end the intolerable circumstance wherein Pennsylvania was one of only nine states not to contribute a dime to pre-kindergarten education. So after months of wrangling with the Republican-controlled legislature, we finally got a budget adopted four days before Christmas. We took care of our deficit by putting together a package of $2.7 billion in tax increases. The only broad-based increase was to our state income tax, which was a flat 2.8 percent, the lowest of any state that had an income tax. We raised it to 3.07 percent and still had the second-lowest state rate. Even though this increase would mean less than $3.15 a week for a family that earned $60,000, it caused an uproar, and my favorable rating dropped significantly. Three years later candidate Swann made this the overriding issue in the reelection campaign. He attacked me for what was the second-largest tax increase in the state's history.

So how, in the face of this, did we win a landslide 20-point victory? Because we did two important things: we invested in progress that made a measurable and significant impact in improving the quality of the lives of our citizens, and we eliminated waste and increased productivity, driving down the cost of operating the government.

Then we used the campaign to let the voters know this and how an engaged, active government could cut costs and invest in making positive change happen. As we rolled out accomplishments, our lead grew and grew.

Over the next four years, as I promised in my victory speech, we gave Pennsylvanians more of the same. For my first six years in office we used the cost savings we effectuated, nearly a $2-billion-a-year reduction, to reinvest in progress that produced such benefit and growth. When the recession hit, we had to tighten our belts and use the cost savings to help balance our budget and offset our precipitous decline in revenue. But even in these two years we continued to increase funding for K–12 education (by $300 million in 2009 and

$250 million in 2010). We were the only state in the nation to make substantial increases in education in the face of the recession. Most states substantially cut education funding.

But our investment in K–12 education, like all of our investments, paid off big-time. Over my eight years as governor we increased education funding by more than $4 billion, not by giving school districts a blank check but by investing money in targeted programs that have a proven track record of success. Programs such as quality pre-K, full-day kindergarten, smaller class sizes, after-school tutoring, hands-on science projects, teacher training, and technology in the classrooms. Over eight years the results were incredible. A total of 290,000 more students were proficient in both reading and math in 2010 than there were in 2002. In 2009 the Center on Education Policy, a Washington, DC, think tank, found that in the previous eight years Pennsylvania was the only state whose students made substantial progress in the national tests at every grade level and in every subject tested. Best of all, in 2010 our eighth-graders ranked first in their reading scores. *U.S. News & World Report* ranked us the fourth-best state for public education.

By investing significant resources in economic development and in our infrastructure we successfully fueled economic growth. In my ninety-six months as governor, Pennsylvania had a lower unemployment rate than the national rate and had the best rate of the industrial states. In years three, four, and five we ranked in the top five in new business attractions and expansions. Even in the teeth of the recession we had a better economy than virtually every other large industrial state. In 2010 we were eleventh in the country in our rate of job growth. The nearest other industrial state placed twenty-ninth. When I left office our unemployment rate was 7.4 percent, almost two points lower than the national average and several points lower than in most other industrial states.

Over my time in office we became a leader in the creation of green-energy jobs. We did so by investing nearly $1 billion as incentive for renewable- and alternative-energy companies. We passed aggressive advanced energy portfolio standards that created a mandate for these new forms of energy. The Pew Center for the States found that we were third in the country, behind only Texas and California.

We made similar progress in strengthening our safety net, protecting our environment, expanding our prescription drug program for our seniors, and increasing research and innovation in the private sector and throughout our universities and medical centers. We did all this by increasing spending and borrowing. Yes, we increased spending and borrowing, and it paid off. And because of our successes in reducing the cost of operations of the government, we were still ranked by the *Wall Street Journal* in 2010 as the seventh most fiscally stable state in the Union. The study found that only ten states were worthy of that designation, with Pennsylvania as the only industrial state and the only eastern state that had maintained fiscal stability.

What we accomplished in Pennsylvania—investing in our growth by increased spending and prudent borrowing while cutting costs—was not unique. It's been done in other states and cities, and it should serve as a blueprint for our federal government as it faces the need to reduce the ballooning deficit and a continuing need to keep investing to promote growth through innovation, education, and infrastructure. Yes, we can do both! It's a clear lesson from the experience that we and other states and cities have had. And this belief was reinforced by the preliminary recommendation of the Simpson-Bowles Deficit Commission, which was commissioned by President Obama and laid out a blueprint for cutting the deficit while investing in growth.

And, of course, there is another equally important lesson that should be learned from my experience as governor. It's okay to raise taxes if by doing so you improve outcomes for people. Politicians are always underestimating the people. People are generally quite reasonable and are supportive of government investing resources if they get a return on the investment. Raising taxes isn't a guaranteed death sentence!

In their hearts most politicians know it's necessary to spend money if it's spent wisely and efficiently, but they are simply too afraid to vote for additional spending and tax increases to support it. Political courage is in short supply at a time when America needs it most. Our leaders won't take risks, nor will they trust the people enough to tell them the truth.

They seem to believe that the American people "can't handle the truth," as Jack Nicholson said in *A Few Good Men*. It all is very circular. We have become, in great part, a nation of wusses, and our leaders are, naturally, the leading wusses. We are afraid to tell each other the truth, we take almost no risks, and, not surprisingly, we make no progress and we are in real danger of losing our place as the leading economy in the world. The nation that was built by risk-takers has become timid, scared, and risk-averse. American progress, which always has seemed almost inevitable, has ground to a halt. It shouldn't be a surprise to us, because no risk usually means no progress. In fact, one of my favorite sayings that accurately sums up our plight is "Behold the turtle, who only makes progress when he sticks his neck out!" Okay, Americans, on the count of ten, let's start stretching those necks out!

CHAPTER 15

How Two Young Non-Wuss Pittsburgh Women Stared Down the Haitian and US Governments

A few short days after the devastating 2010 earthquake had hit and almost leveled Haiti, I received a call from Leslie Merrill, one of my Pittsburgh supporters who worked for the University of Pittsburgh Medical Center (UPMC). She told me that they had been contacted by the family of two young Pittsburgh women, Jamie and Alison McMutrie, who had been working at an orphanage in Port-au-Prince. The orphanage's buildings had been almost totally destroyed, the senior staff had left, and the sisters were living on the sidewalk outside the buildings with 150 children. They needed help—medical personnel, medical supplies, food, and water—but most of all they wanted to take the 54 children who had been cleared for adoption out of Haiti. They had already been approved for adoption in the United States, Canada, or Spain; most of them had specific families who had been cleared to take them.

UPMC was organizing a trip to send some of its medical personnel and desperately needed medicines and supplies to Haiti. Republic Airlines had donated a very big plane and crew for their use, but they couldn't get clearance to land. So Leslie, believing that as governor I could do anything, called me for help. I didn't have a clue. I made a few calls to US officials but got nowhere. Then on a Saturday morning Leslie saw the Haitian ambassador to the United States, Ray Joseph, being interviewed on CNN. She called me and asked me to try to call him. She felt like he was a decent and honorable man (it turned out he was that and much more—a real hero in this story).

I spraung into action. I called my contacts at CNN and got his cell phone number. I reached him and related the story and our twofold goal. First, to bring three thousand pounds of supplies to the stricken island, and second, to take the sisters and the orphans back to the United States and to the loving families waiting for them. The ambassador swung into action, and the UPMC folks were cleared to go to Port-au-Prince on Monday, January 18. Ambassador Joseph asked me if I was going and I said "no." I didn't want to look like a grandstanding politician, and I didn't believe I would be of any use down there. The ambassador said, "No, Governor, you have to go. It is almost certain that sometime during this trip they will need your clout to get things accomplished or to get out of trouble—you have to go."

Although I knew the press would give me grief for this, I knew the ambassador was probably right, so I decided to go. I asked my wife, Midge, to go with me. I knew she would be moved by the experience, but I also knew that as a federal appellate court judge she would add clout if we needed it. I also wanted her along because she has incredible judgment and common sense and because she is always amazingly calm under pressure—the latter a quality I don't have and I felt we would surely need.

Midge and I talked on Sunday about the trip and what supplies we might need. We figured the orphans, many of whom were less than two years of age and some as old as fourteen, would be hungry, thirsty, scared, and need things to occupy them on a long flight to Pittsburgh (we were planning to take them back to Pittsburgh because Leslie had arranged for the UPMC's Children's Hospital to take them in until their new parents came to get them). So we purchased soda, water, juice, cookies, snacks, books, and toys en masse. The two of us and my state police detail carted out from a Dollar Store bags and bags of supplies, all of which turned out to be very useful.

Midge and I flew to Pittsburgh on Monday on the state plane and we boarded a chartered jet with the UPMC folks—mostly doctors and nurses—and off we went. Hours later we approached the only working airport in Port-au-Prince; the airport was being run by the US military. We circled for what seemed like an eternity, and finally one of the pilots came out and said we were being denied permission to land. He asked me if he could tell the officials that I was aboard, and I said "sure." He did, and magically we were cleared to land. It didn't take long for Ambassador Joseph's admonition to me to be proven accurate. We landed at about 6:00 P.M. and were in Haiti for the next five hours.

When we deplaned, all hell broke loose. We were in touch with Jamie and Ali, and they had gotten two large vans and hoped to go directly to meet us at the airport. I was in touch with State Department officials back in Washington and the military commanders at the airfield. There were all sorts of resistance to letting the children go back with us. It looked like our mission was doomed. We had an order from a Haitian judge that said the children living in Bresma (where the orphanage was) could be taken out of the country to a place where they could be safe. However, when the vans reached the US embassy, we were told that fourteen of the fifty-four children had not been formally adopted and that they would not be permitted to leave. The other forty would. I thought we should consider ourselves lucky and leave immediately with the forty. But the two sisters from Pittsburgh, who were the antitheses of wusses, said "no." They said that we are a family and that none of the children is leaving unless they all go.

We were at a stalemate. Leslie and Midge were at the US embassy dealing with Haitian and US officials, who weren't budging, and I was talking to US military personnel (who were great) and eventually to Dennis McDonough from the National Security Council, who appeared to be the American in charge at the airport. The stalemate lasted for hours and finally the military officials ordered our plane to take off. (Because so many planes were coming into Haiti and they needed tarmac space, they limited planes to two hours on the ground. We had gotten about four hours but couldn't get any longer.) I panicked. How were we going to get the children to Pittsburgh? The military personnel said not to worry; they would work it out. We were talking to State Department, Homeland Security, and White House officials, and Donna Cooper, my secretary of policy, was working the phones back in Harrisburg. Donna received an e-mail from Homeland Security saying we couldn't take the fourteen undocumented children out. I was personally talking to Huma Abedin, Secretary of State Clinton's closest aide.

It seemed that this deadlock lasted for an eternity. It was like an episode from *Mission Impossible*. So much tension and conflict. I was shouting over a cell phone at Washington officials saying people are starving here, literally dying in the streets, kids are being taken hostage by bad guys, we have an order from a Haitian judge— what in God's name is wrong with the US government, are we so bureaucratic we can't make a decision to save these kids? I didn't seem to be getting through.

But sometime after ten o'clock a miracle happened. Dennis McDonough, who was on the phone with Rahm Emanuel, then the White House chief of staff, ended his conversation and told us that all fifty-four kids could go to the United States.

How did it happen? To be honest, I can't really say. It may have been the constant pressure that Donna Cooper and I put on them, our consistent pounding of officials in State, Homeland Security, and the White House, but I doubt it. It may have been that someone in Washington decided not to be a wuss and save those desperate, innocent orphans, but that would be a real departure from the norm. I am not certain, but if I had to guess it may have been a result of the president's health care bill. Huh? Well, let me explain. Passing the Affordable Care Act was the White House's number-one priority. Congressman Jason Altmire was a suburban Pittsburgh Democrat who was on the fence regarding the bill. He was with us on the plane, but hadn't been much of a help for the first four hours or so. But then we encouraged him to call the White House, and he did. If I had to guess, that's what did it. It was probably politics, not humanitarian concerns, that won the day. Hey, whatever works!

Minutes after Dennis McDonough told us that everyone could go, Lieutenant Colonel Randon Draper, who had been great, told me they were flying an empty C-17 cargo plane back to Sanford Air Force Base in Orlando and that we could hitch a ride on it. "We" were fifty-four Haitian kids, medical personnel from UPMC, Leslie, her son Herbie, Midge, and me. We had no idea how we would get from Florida back to Pittsburgh, but being intrepid non-wusses, we said, "Great!"

So we loaded up the C-17. It was a sight to see. A C-17 is as big as a football field and is mostly empty space inside, waiting to be filled with cargo. There are benches on each side that can seat about sixty people each. We had fifty-four kids and about sixty-five adults. At ten forty-five we were ready to go. Ali and Jamie took one last head count and found that we didn't have fifty-four kids on board, only fifty-three. A second head count revealed that we were missing Emma, a two-year-old girl (Emma was my mom's name, so I will never forget her).

Things got crazy. The military personnel were telling us we had to leave, but the sisters refused to go without all fifty-four. There was a lot of shouting and plenty of tears. I finally persuaded the sisters that the military was going to fly the plane out and the best course of action would be for one of them to stay behind and look for Emma. Jamie volunteered. So shortly after eleven o'clock we rolled out for takeoff. We had been on the ground in

Haiti for only five hours, but it seemed like it had been days. What a sight we were. Fifty-three Haitian kids, most of whom were sitting on the laps of people they had met only an hour before, and one governor, who had no seat and was crouching on some cargo bags in the middle of the plane and holding onto a strap for dear life. As the plane started up, the noise was deafening. It should have been terrifying to those kids, who had never been on an airplane before. But it wasn't. They sat there calmly, almost happily. They were on this huge, cavernous plane, leaving a place where they had lived all their lives, going to a place they had never even been before to live the rest of their lives. They were amazing! All throughout this ordeal they had been terrific. When Midge, Leslie, and her son Herbie met them on the vans at our embassy the Haitian kids were singing gospel songs like it was an ordinary Sunday. They never betrayed any fear. Haiti still has a long way to go in its recovery and the world needs to continue to help make that possible, but if these young children are typical Haitians, then their faith and spirit will someday prevail.

The plane trip was remarkably uneventful. Midge and I played the part of flight attendants. We went up and down the aisle distributing juice, soda, and snacks. The kids gobbled them up. The coloring books and toys we had bought on Sunday night at the Dollar Store were also hits, especially with the younger kids. I later told people that I had walked from Haiti to Orlando. This experience gave me a great appreciation for how hard flight attendants work, but I loved every minute of it.

We got to Sanford Air Force Base, and the plane was boarded by armed customs police. I thought we were all going to be arrested. I talked to their supervisor and assured him that the Haitian kids all had visas (formally given to them grudgingly by customs officials) and that Ali had all their adoption documentation. I said that on faith. I had no idea if she did, but she came through like a champ. She had boxes of paperwork, which she showed immigration officials in a painstaking process that took nearly five hours.

In the meantime, the kids were packed into a room, but their eyes were filled with wonder because they were watching cartoons on DVDs. They didn't seem tired or scared at all. Midge and some of the medical personnel formed a diaper brigade—they must have changed tons of dirty diapers—while Ali labored with the immigration officials. During the trip we had to deal with a number of immigration officials, and they were great. They weren't wuss bureaucrats, and they understood the unique situation they were dealing with. They didn't exactly bend the rules, but they stretched them a bit. Their boss, Alejandro Mayorkas, was also great throughout the whole adventure. We wouldn't have been successful without him.

In addition to working out the kinks with Immigration and taking care of the diaper challenge, we needed to find a way to get from Orlando to Pittsburgh. We couldn't find commercial flights for all of us, so we needed a plane. That's easy. All we had to do was find a plane and a crew at 1:30 A.M. I tried reaching my contacts in the airlines, but not a chance at that hour. It looked hopeless, but Leslie pulled off another miracle. She got a plane from the COO of Republic Airlines, but we needed to find a crew to fly it. With Republic's help we located our original crew in Miami, where they had gotten just enough rest under FAA regulations so they could fly us to Pittsburgh.

While all this was going on, we received great news—Jamie had found Emma! She had fallen asleep on a couch at the US embassy, slept right through, and didn't board one of the vans to go to the airport. Now we had to find a way to get Emma and Jamie home from Port-au-Prince. I called and called everyone and finally got US Airways to agree to give them safe and free passage to Pittsburgh.

We finally took off for Pittsburgh at about seven o'clock in the morning. We were all dog tired but had a great feeling of accomplishment.

When we landed in Pittsburgh another amazing thing happened—it was snowing! Snow in January in America's most livable city is not unusual for us, but for the Haitian children it was an incredible sight. They deplaned with wonder in their eyes and smiles on their faces as they saw for the first time the white stuff that we take for granted.

Also, during the flights, I'd became more convinced than ever that Jason Altmire's potential health care vote was probably behind the help we'd gotten. I had received several calls from White House officials while we were still on the ground in Port-au-Prince and then when we landed on US soil, asking me to give credit to Jason at the press conference we would hold when we finally landed in Pittsburgh. I did because he deserved it, but in one of those ironies that so often happens in politics, Jason would eventually vote no on the health care bill!

When we came home we faced great jubilation, especially from the Haitian American community, but as they say, "no good deed goes unpunished," and we were criticized as well. Anderson Cooper of CNN, as I had feared, attacked me as a grandstanding pol who had thrown his weight around to take a few Haitian children out while many others were not permitted to leave. He said we had received special treatment. But I figure, thank God *someone* got special treatment. These fifty-four orphans had escaped desperate conditions and were going to be adopted by loving families.

In fact, after the euphoria of this amazing journey had worn off, the bureaucratic morass set in. The kids were housed in the short run at the Children's Institute in Pittsburgh. Over a few weeks time the adoptive parents came and picked up the forty-two kids whose adoption papers had been formalized, but the other twelve were kept there for what felt like forever. It took about a year for them to finally leave the institute and go to their new families. In fact, it was heartbreaking that the US and Haitian governments couldn't agree on an expedited process to get orphaned Haitian kids who had no family and no future on the island to America, where tens of thousands of willing parents were ready to adopt them and give them loving homes. In every bureaucracy there is a standard way of doing things. And anything that doesn't follow that standard way gets delayed, put in a corner, walled off, and ignored. No one wants to take responsibility for doing anything outside the norm, even when it's clearly the right thing to do.

Finally the logjam was broken by a caring Republican congressman, Jeff Fortenberry from Nebraska, who got legislation passed that cleared away the roadblocks.

This almost interminable delay caused by wuss bureaucrats in both countries didn't spoil what we had done. We accomplished this with help from a lot of great people who made it happen: US and Haitian government officials, folks from Republic Airlines and US Airways, the incredibly adept problem solvers in the US military, and the great medical personnel from UPMC and other hospitals. It shows what can happen when we want to make it happen. As for me, it was an incredible adventure. We accomplished so much in fewer than twenty-four hours (I was back in Harrisburg before noon on Tuesday). I can't think of any one thing I have done in my political career that brought me more satisfaction and pure joy. When I watched those fifty-three kids (no Emma) deplane in Pittsburgh I was crying, but they truly were tears of joy. In the past two years I have heard from many of the adoptive families and even gotten to see Midge's Alex, an infant who had flown on her lap from Haiti to Sanford and then from Sanford to Pittsburgh. He was adopted by a family from Kansas, but the wife was from suburban Philadelphia, and when they were here visiting her parents we met and took Alex to Franklin Square in Philadelphia. As for the sisters, they went back to Haiti to work with other kids and to help that embattled country on its long recovery. I had a chance to salute them in front of the Pennsylvania legislature when I gave my 2010 budget address. They came to the Capitol and received a standing ovation for their courage, their unwillingness to settle, and for their "non-wuss" spirit.

CHAPTER 16

Sports and Politics

I have always loved sports. That was another passion I got from my dad in the fourteen years we had together. He took me and my brother Robert (three years older and much smarter than I; he's now an international tax lawyer in Dallas) to countless baseball and football games and turned us into diehard Giant fans in both sports. We had two tickets for football Giant games, and he would take me to one game and Robert to the next. He died on December 4, 1958, and Robert and I took the two tickets to the Giants-Colts NFL Championship game on December 28, 1958, which some people say was the greatest football game ever played. It was exciting as all get-out, but it was tinged with melancholy and sadness for Robert and me as we sat in our seats without him.

I was reminded of that some fifty-one years later when I bet the governor of Arizona, Jan Brewer, on who would win the 2009

Super Bowl, the Arizona Cardinals or the Pittsburgh Steelers. We had bet a trip for two for the winning state, to either Phoenix or Pittsburgh. The Steelers won and I had to decide how to pick two Pittsburghers to win the trip. We created a contest for a 250-word essay titled "Why I Love the Steelers." We received fourteen hundred entries and I read the top-ten-rated essays and had to pick a winner. I thought it would be tough, but it turned out to be easy. The winner wrote that his love of the Steelers went back to going to their games when he was young with his dad. The Steelers were woeful for the early years of his life, but when he was sixteen they made it to the AFC Championship game, which was to be played in Pittsburgh. His dad could get only one ticket, but on the day of the game they both went down to the stadium certain that they could scalp an extra ticket. They couldn't find a single one to buy—no one was selling. So his dad told him to take their one ticket and go to the game. He refused, however, and he wrote that he told his dad, "Dad, I have a hunch the Steelers are going to be good for many years to come and I'll have plenty of chances to see them in title games. You go." His dad did and the Steelers won. He was overjoyed to have been there, but three months later he died of a heart attack. As I read his essay, I began to cry, thinking of my dad. Well, he and his son went off to vacation in Arizona courtesy of the State Tourism Bureau and those great Pittsburgh Steelers.

My love of and knowledge about sports have been real assets to me in my political career most of the time. The more my passion for local teams and my knowledge of the nuances of the games became known, the more I became a "regular guy" in the voters' minds, which helped to deflect any image of an elite, Ivy League–educated lawyer.

It all started during my early years as mayor, when I began to call into the Angelo Cataldi morning sports talk show on WIP radio. For almost two decades it has been as popular with as large an audience as any sports talk radio station in the country. I would call in periodically and joke and talk about whatever news was going on in the Philadelphia sports world. Angelo has a great sense of humor and we had great chemistry, and it was always fun. People would stop me on the streets and say, "Hey, I heard you on Angelo this morning. You are dead right about Reggie White."

That was the first sports controversy I got embroiled in. Our owner, Norman Braman, did not want to re-sign White, a great defensive end for the Eagles, because Norman said he was asking for too much money. Reggie was not only the best defensive end in football, he also was the emotional leader of our defense (something the front office was not factoring in), and he was a great part of the Philadelphia community. He and his wife, Sara, worked tirelessly to create quality housing and learning opportunities for poorer Philadelphians. I felt that his loss would be a catastrophe for our team and the city. So Angelo and I led a campaign to pressure the Eagles to re-sign Reggie. We held a rally attended by more than a thousand people, agitated daily, and then I made the mistake of asking fans to call the Eagles and gave out a private number, which then received thousands of calls. It took years before Norman, who soon after sold the team, would forgive me.

In 1998 I got a call from someone at Comcast Spectacor inquiring whether I had any interest in being on a panel after every Eagles game; the panel would talk about the game and where the Eagles' season appeared to be headed. They said they would pay me, but I felt that as mayor, though such payment would not be illegal, it might appear to be inappropriate. So I asked if it could be directed to charity, and they said "yes." (I should note that today as a civilian I no longer deem it inappropriate, and I direct it to my bank account.)

I knew it would create a bit of trouble for me. Veteran sportswriters were outraged that an "outsider" who they said knew nothing about sports would be allowed to be an "analyst" on TV. Of course, they weren't listening. I never said I was an expert, but that I was a fan and that I would try (and I have tried) to give the fans' perspective and ask questions the fans were wondering about. Besides, we had an expert on the show in Ray Didinger, a

Hall of Fame sportswriter, and we always had an ex-Eagle to give the players' view.

When I was governor, the Republicans lit into me for taking time away from my job. These hypocrites, who spent hours playing rounds of golf, criticized me for spending ninety minutes on the show each week. I told the press that on Sundays when we mostly do the show you could shoot a machine gun down the halls of the Capitol without fear of hitting anyone, and that was the truth.

I even got criticized by Donovan McNabb, although maybe I deserved it from him. When I was Democratic Party chairman in 2000, the *New York Times* did a feature in its sports section about my broadcasting work, and they asked Donovan to critique it. He replied, "He's a very good mayor." They then asked him specifically about my talent as a football analyst and he said, "He's a very good mayor." Our relationship got off to a rocky start when I publically urged the Eagles to take Ricky Williams in the draft where they selected Donovan. I like to think his appreciation for my football insight improved as I became a consistent supporter of his—something many Philadelphians have never let me forget.

I am certain that the benefits I have received from doing the show have far outweighed the drawbacks. First and foremost, I just love doing it. It's also a great way for me to deal with the stress my jobs have given me. During a tough week I would always look forward to Sunday—watching the Birds and doing the show. For these reasons I want to keep doing it as long as CSN will have me, and that's why I once said that even if I were elected president, I would keep doing it (though I don't think the Secret Service would be happy about the pregame shows outside the stadium).

Most importantly, the show has turned out to be a great political asset. It gets great ratings and is shown all over the eastern half of Pennsylvania. It has helped my reputation as a "regular guy." When I was out at parades or among crowds, people would ask me as much about the Eagles and sports in general as they would taxes or education. When I announced my candidacy for governor early in 2002, I did a fly-around to the state's six media markets. I was in Wilkes-Barre, and after a press conference we walked across the town square to eat at a famous hot dog place. As we got to the door an elderly couple was coming out and the wife said, "Are you Mayor Rendell?" When I said I was, she pointed to her husband and said, "*He's* voting for you [implying that she wasn't]. He thought you were a good mayor, but the real reason he's voting for you is that he loves that football show."

A place where sports and politics often overlap is the dreaded Opening Day first pitch. All politicians must deal with the thorny issue of throwing out the first ball to open up the baseball season. It's an enticing invitation to receive. The politician thinks "this will make me look like a real person and a true sports fan." Wrong; it almost never turns out well.

Let's examine the reasons.

1. You Almost Always Get Booed

It really doesn't matter how well you are doing your job or how popular you are, it seems to be a great American pastime to boo politicians on Opening Day or at any other sports event.

I have never thrown out the first ball at a Phillies game, but I have at numerous minor league games throughout Pennsylvania—and consistently been booed. In the spring of 2010, I was asked to throw out the first ball at the opening of the Harrisburg Senators' beautiful stadium—and I was booed. Good grief, I signed off on $17 million to help make that stadium a reality, and they still booed me!

In 1995 I won reelection as mayor with 80 percent of the vote, but a few days later I was booed at a soccer game. In 2005, after losing a bet with then-governor Mitt Romney over the Patriots-Eagles Super Bowl (thank goodness it wasn't for $10,000, right?), I was booed at halftime of a Celtics-Sixers game in Boston. Of course that was because I was the loser of the bet, so I had to sing the national anthem during halftime of the game. I was with Midge, who is a great singer, and after I wailed out a few verses and got booed, she stepped in and the crowd went wild. Singing isn't my strong suit, and I deserved to be booed that day.

There was only one time I went on the field and participated in a ceremony and didn't get booed. That was in 1993, when the "everyman Phils" made it to the World Series. I was asked to conduct the Philadelphia Orchestra in playing the national anthem. I actually was cheered, but to tell the truth, our fans were so delirious over unexpectedly being in the World Series that they would have cheered Hannibal Lecter.

2. You Will Almost Always Look Like a Doofus

When you throw out the first ball, you must wrestle with the question "What will I wear?" There is no right answer. If you put on team paraphernalia, the fans hate it. They simply don't like pols wearing team garb, especially if they feel that he or she is not a real fan and is just doing it for publicity. Second, rarely does an elected official look good in team clothes. We're out of shape and look anything but authentic.

A few years ago, the mayor of Philadelphia, Michael Nutter (whom I like and respect), threw out the first pitch at a Phillies game. He wasn't content to wear a Phils hat and jacket, he wanted to don the genuine Phillies uniform—shirt, pants, hat, socks, and spikes. That would have been a complete disaster.

The mayor, a man who usually possesses class and dignity, would have looked like a brown-nosing weenie. Fortunately, the Phils' management talked him out of it and he wore a hat and jersey, thereby only looking like half a weenie.

You also can enrage fans if you don the other team's stuff. President Obama has urged us to do big, bold, and brave things as a nation, and he has demonstrated that same bravery by wearing a hat or a jacket of his beloved White Sox no matter what city he is in to throw out the first ball.

3. The Chance of Your Throwing a Good Pitch Is Almost Nil

The best reasons for politicians to stay away from first-pitch invitations is that they will surely throw the ball into the ground or too wide or too high.

After accepting an invitation to throw out the first ball, the politician and his or her staff will have arduous practice sessions (e.g., Martin Sheen in *The West Wing*). In won't help! I've done it both ways—lots of practice or just going up there cold—I still have never thrown a strike. I've put them in the ground, over the catcher's head, wide left, wide right. I've tried throwing hard and straight or rainbowing it. No difference. I sucked either way.

My only consolation is that I'm not the only one who sucks. There is a long line of celebrity first pitchers who were awful, too. If fact, if you're interested in viewing the "ten worst ceremonial first pitches," go to YouTube.

The number-one worst pitch, according to that list, was thrown by Mariah Carey, but given the tightness of her clothes, that's not a surprise. I think the worst was from Mayor Mark Mallory of Cincinnati; he couldn't have done worse if he were trying. Number eight was thrown by a mascot, a *Tyrannosaurus rex*. Actually, I feel it shouldn't have been on the list because the *T. rex* has tiny arms and it couldn't bend down far enough to pick up the ball, so it actually threw the ball with its mouth and came closer to the plate than the mayor.

There is one sports stadium in which I've never been booed and that's the Palestra, the University of Pennsylvania's basketball arena, the oldest basketball arena in the nation. I've been going to the Palestra since the winter of 1961. I am a loyal Penn alumnus and try to attend every home game. (I even did as governor, and, for those of you weak on geography, Harrisburg is where the governor's mansion is, ninety-eight miles from Philadelphia.) The Palestra is my refuge. The people there respect my status as a fan and leave me alone, almost never asking me about issues or for help. The worst I get is to be asked for an autograph or for a picture, and that stuff is fun.

In fifty years of going to the Palestra only once has my sanctuary been violated. That occurred in 1992, and it couldn't have happened at a worse time. It was my first year as mayor, and as I've related we had to cut almost every one of our programs. I was going to the Palestra to attend a Penn-Yale game with Jesse, who was twelve at the time. At about three-thirty my office reception area was invaded by a group of protesters, all of whom were in wheelchairs. They were agitated by our refusal to do curb cuts at the corner of every street in which we had done pothole repair. We simply couldn't afford to do it and it would be absurd to be forced to do curb cuts on streets that had no sidewalks. I have great empathy with the challenges of our disabled citizens so it was difficult for me to oppose their requests, but our budget and common sense dictated that I do so.

The protesters then did something shocking. They got out of their wheelchairs and lay on the floor. They stayed there and wouldn't move. (Agree or disagree with their cause, you have to admire the guts that took.) At six-thirty I had to leave to meet my son at the Palestra. My security detail asked me if I wanted to go out the side door, which would have allowed me to avoid seeing them. That would have been wussing out, so I went out through the reception room and tried to explain to them the reasons behind our decision. It didn't go well and I wound up arguing vehemently with my friends lying on the floor—as depressing an encounter as I could remember.

But I was off to the Palestra, where things would be better, where I could look forward to a peaceful, non-eventful Penn victory. Wrong! Almost ten minutes after the game started I looked up and in the last three rows behind a basket I saw some people unfolding rollouts. Rollouts are a Palestra tradition—they are signs that when unrolled have some fun and witty message such as "the Princeton Tiger is a toothless tabby" (actually the kids are a lot funnier than that). It appears that there were going to be three rollouts, one on each row. As soon as the first rollout began to unfold I knew I was in trouble. It read, "Who could be mean enough"—it had to be me, but in the Palestra? The second row read, "To close a library used by kids," and, of course, the third row, "Mayor Rendell!"

I knew when I took over as mayor in January 1992 that I would have to make some hard cuts, and I was ready to deal with the pain because I believed that our long-run plan would allow us to replenish those cuts and invest even more, but the back-to-back run-ins with the disabled and the library folks (by the way, the library was in a rented building, and of more than seventy branches, it had the lowest use) were as depressing as anything I have ever felt in my thirty-three years in government.

Though my passion for sports has been a great asset to me, there were a few times when it presented me with a real challenge. The first was in late 2004, when the Eagles and the Steelers were in their conference championship games and there was a real chance there would be a Philadelphia vs. Pittsburgh Super Bowl. The same scenario presented itself in 2008, when both teams were again in their conference championship games.

To understand why this presented a problem for me, you must know the political landscape in the great commonwealth of Pennsylvania. Start with the proposition that virtually everyone in the state dislikes Philadelphia for a whole host of reasons, some real and some imagined. Combine that with the fact that Pittsburgh, the state's second-largest city, is always saying that Philadelphia gets too much money, too much attention, too much everything. So as it appeared that the Steelers and the Eagles were fated to face each other in the Super Bowl, the question was asked over and over again, who was the governor, the former mayor of

Philadelphia, going to root for? This presented a great challenge for me in 2005, when I knew I had to run for reelection in one year, and the rumor was that my opponent would be the charismatic former Steeler great Lynn Swann.

What should I do? Should I wuss out and take the safe route by saying that I would be neutral, just rooting for a great game? Or should I tell the truth and say that I'm an Eagles fan and it's the Birds all the way? I decided I had stood tall and shown courage on raising taxes, gay rights, gun control, and other controversial issues, so I could be strong once again. There was no way I was going to wuss out on my beloved Eagles.

So I answered the question that I was rooting for both the Steelers and the Eagles to win their conference championships, but if they did I would root for the Eagles in the Super Bowl. In Pittsburgh I tried to explain by asking Steeler fans how they would feel if a former Pittsburgh mayor who had been a thirty-year Steeler season ticket holder became governor and said that he was neutral in a Steelers-Eagles battle. It worked with real Steeler fans, who understood what being a real fan means. They would have lost respect for me if I waffled. My problem was with the casual bandwagon jumper, who wasn't a longtime fan. For them it was a case of me favoring Philadelphia "again," which I never did as governor on real issues.

As it turned out, fate let me escape from the real horror because the Eagles won in 2004 and went to the 2005 Super Bowl, but the Steelers lost to the Patriots and in 2008 the Steelers won, but the Eagles fell to the Cardinals. Actually, I always hoped for a Steelers-Eagles Super Bowl. It would be a hoot! The host city would be leveled by the combination of rabid Steeler and Eagle fans. And best of all, the traditional bet made between the governors of both teams would be me betting against myself. I would have had great fun with that, but alas, it wasn't to be.

By the way, in my 2006 election versus Lynn Swann I carried both the city of Pittsburgh and its surrounding Allegheny County. So I guess my honest answer was accepted by most Pittsburghers. A real victory for non-wusses everywhere!

CHAPTER 17

"Like a Sturgeon"

I t was late on a Wednesday afternoon in 2009 and I was at a
meeting in Senator Specter's office regarding the potential
dredging of the Delaware River to a depth of forty-five feet. This
was essential if the port of Philadelphia was to stay competitive,
because the new giant cargo ships were being built so big that we
could not accommodate them at our current depth of forty feet.
At forty-five feet we would be highly competitive, and this could
create thousands of longshoremen and trucking jobs. These jobs
are vital to any region because they are among the only jobs that
pay $70,000 to $90,000 a year and can be held by those without
a high school diploma but who have a strong back and a strong
work ethic.

That afternoon we were trying to persuade the Army Corps of
Engineers to begin the dredging process. To say that the corps was

reluctant was an understatement. Senator Specter was on our side, and at my request he had convened a meeting to help persuade the corps.

The room was packed, with an assistant secretary of the army from the corps who had the power to make this decision, and representatives from the Environmental Protection Agency, the Justice Department, the coast guard, and the National Oceanic and Atmospheric Administration (NOAA).

The issue was whether dredging could begin without the corps obtaining a new Environmental Impact Statement (EIS) or Environmental Assessment (EA). An EIS is the more extensive study that is required under the National Environmental Policy Act. Since 1992, two EIS's had been done on the project, along with three economic studies and countless environmental monitoring studies by the corps between 1997 and 2007. Nonetheless, the Justice Department and NOAA representatives were pushing hard for another study, though a lawyer on Senator Specter's staff was pushing back effectively on every point they were trying to make. This was a crucial issue, because if the corps ordered an EIS to be done, it would delay dredging by at least two years. I knew that another delay would be fatal to the project, but because Senator Specter's lawyer was doing so well, I sat there observing, with uncharacteristic silence.

A politician running for office can often win a lot of people over by saying he will never compromise. But that's the easy way out. Compromise is hard; negotiating isn't easy. Saying no to everything—often leaving the problem for someone else to solve—is nice and simple. When you're in charge of anything, from a small business to president of the United States, you're going to find yourself in situations like this. Every person in that room was operating in good faith, armed with solid research, based on important principles all Americans share, and they didn't agree. Still, a decision had to be made, and we had to make sure it was the right one.

The main point that the Justice Department and NOAA representatives were making was that a large school of sturgeon had just recently (for the past three years) begun to populate the stretch of the Delaware River where dredging would occur. The dredging process could kill or injure them, disrupting their habitat at the very least. At this point the meeting had lasted for more than two hours, and I silently began doodling. Almost reflexively, I wrote these words on a blank piece of paper:

"Like a sturgeon, touched for the very first time."

I handed the paper to BJ Clark, my aide who was working on the project, and I could see he was struggling to keep from losing it.

The debate raged on and finally I spoke up. I began by stating that I had as much regard for the noble sturgeon as anyone, but I noted that if they had been populating that stretch of the river, then they had been exposed to dredging because we have to dredge every year to maintain our forty-foot depth and take out the silt and debris that have built up. I asked the NOAA folks if they had found any dead sturgeon and they replied, "No, in fact the school has grown in numbers every year."

Aha! Got you! "The sturgeon like dredging. They really like it." Well, like it or not, it hadn't hurt them in the past. The corps decided to proceed. After leaving the senator's office, flushed with victory, I reflected on my previous government experience and realized that I had fought similar battles before.

It was 1992, my first year in office, and the challenge we were facing was enormous. We had a $250 million deficit, 13 percent of our total budget. Our capital budget had shrunk to nearly $25 million. We couldn't invest in anything, even the maintenance of our buildings. We couldn't buy anything. Our vendors were threatening to cut us off (including the loss of toilet paper for City Hall, a potential tragedy of colossal proportions).

About two months on the job and we were all occupied with working feverishly to find ways to cut out waste, increase production, and manage more effectively to try to eat away at our immense deficit. In the middle of all this, my water commissioner, Kumar Kishinchand, told me some unbelievable news: the Delaware River Basin Commission was about to order us to build a tertiary treatment plant on the Delaware River. Projected costs would be $120 million of capital investment and $25 million to $30 million a year to operate. I was stunned. I knew we had primary and secondary treatment plants up and running to try to improve the quality of the river water. How could we possibly need a third? And how could we begin to afford its construction or operation?

The answer to the first question was astonishing. They were ordering us to build the tertiary treatment plant to improve the oxygen content in the water for the fish. I asked in essence the same question I was to ask seventeen years later in Senator Specter's office: "Were the fish dying?" I received the same negative reply, and I went crazy. "If the fish are not dying, how do we know the oxygen content in the water is bad for them? Did we ask them if they were uncomfortable?"

I was so infuriated I told Commissioner Kishinchand that we would refuse to comply. He told me that the basin commission could go to federal court and get an order forcing us to comply. I said, "Tell the commission I still won't comply, and if the judge winds up putting me in jail for contempt, I will end up on the cover of *Time* magazine for being the mayor who went to jail for refusing to spend $125 million of his taxpayers' money to build a third treatment plant to make fish more comfortable." The commission backed down, and the plant was never built.

But believe it or not, that wasn't the silliest order we ever received from a regulator. This time it wasn't environmental. The city of Philadelphia was threatened for violating the Americans with Disabilities Act. Again, this happened early in my first term as mayor. My wonderful Parking Authority director, Rina Cutler, came to me with another unbelievable tale. A Justice Department lawyer was threatening to sue the Parking Authority for not having Braille designations of the floors in the elevator of one of the

Parking Authority's garages. I asked Rina if the lawyer knew that there was no retail above the ground floor, only parking. She said, "yes." Aaaaagh! This can't be true! We're about to be sued for not having Braille in an elevator that goes only to floors where cars are parked. How many unescorted blind persons would have any reason whatsoever to be in that elevator?

I told Rina to tell the Justice Department lawyer to sue us and that I would have a press conference in front of the elevator and explain that this was the stupidest legal action in the history of mankind. Needless to say, no enforcement was ever filed.

Now, don't get me wrong. I am not antiregulation. In fact, most environmental laws and regulations have been godsends, protecting us from pollution and bacteria that can endanger our health and the quality of our lives. But they have to be applied with common sense. There must be a balance. And that is true for all regulations. They must be assessed by a cost-benefit analysis and must allow reasonable growth by business. And even more importantly, our environmental regulations must be enforced far more speedily. Today it takes almost four years to build a new road or bridge. The biggest factor in that terribly long delay is the EIS. It often will take nearly two years to complete. There is simply no excuse for that. The process must be streamlined so it takes less than a year. We can do it. Remember when the bridge collapsed in Minnesota? A new bridge was built in just thirteen months. There was no environmental harm done. We can have good environmental protection and oversight without ridiculous outcomes and without needless delays.

CHAPTER 18

"Hillary, Hillary . . ."

I t was the night of the Salahi dinner at the White House. It was really a state dinner for the president of India, but because of America's most famous gate-crashing couple, it became known as the "Salahi dinner."

We had been invited and were sitting at a table with my friend and colleague Mayor Michael Bloomberg (a truly great leader) and his significant other, the charismatic Diana Taylor. In came Secretary of State Clinton, and she walked to a table right next to ours. She didn't see us and I sneaked up behind her and put my hands on her shoulders and whispered in her ear, "I have one more presidential campaign left in me!"

As you can tell, I really, really like Bill Clinton and think he was the best president in my lifetime, but I love Hillary and think she would have made an even better president. I hope and pray that someday she will.

I got to know Hillary during the campaign of 1992 and the eight years of Bill's presidency. I liked her and admired her then for many reasons. Her passion for fairness and for people, which she demonstrated during the Clintons' ill-fated effort to enact national health care. The class and grace she showed as a senator, by working hard to learn her craft and not presuming that, as a former first lady, she had a special status and was more important than the average senator. Her willingness to be a consummate team player, which she exemplifies daily as President Obama's secretary of state.

All these reasons are why I like her, but I fell in love with her in 2008, during the seven-week Pennsylvania primary campaign, from March 4 to April 22. Few people in Pennsylvania ever believed that our primary would be relevant. It had never been before, because it was far too late on the primary schedule. In fact, I had tried unsuccessfully to move the primary up to, at least, Super Tuesday. Some genius I am. On Super Tuesday, we would have been one of twenty-three other states holding primary elections. Instead, we were the center of the political universe for seven weeks.

How that happened was nothing short of amazing. First, Hillary blew what should have been an insurmountable advantage. Senator Obama pulled off a tremendous upset in Iowa, and Hillary stood on the brink of political extinction. If she lost the New Hampshire primary, the Obama wave would have wiped her out. She was trailing in the polls, and then on the Saturday before the primary, she teared up when she talked about how difficult it is being constantly in the public eye, the demands and the expectations she has to meet, and how frustrating it is to think that she might not be in a position to help people with their problems.

I empathized with her as someone who had been in the public eye for thirty-plus years and had lost two elections. What I didn't realize is how this incident and the derision that was quickly heaped on Hillary by the media would affect women. I soon learned when my wife, Midge, became enraged at the way the media made fun of Hillary for tearing up. Midge had always admired Hillary, but this was something different. Midge was furious at what she believed (and I agreed) was unfair treatment of Hillary by the media because she was a woman. I was truly surprised because I never knew Midge felt so deeply about this, given the meteoric rise of her career, breaking one glass ceiling after another. Midge was only the second woman made partner by her prestigious Philadelphia law firm, was appointed a federal district court judge in 1994, and was elevated to a federal court of appeals four years later because of her work on the district court. Yet she, too, had felt the slings and arrows that some men visit on women who pursue careers. She was angry, and little did any of the experts and pollsters realize that many other women were as well. There were a number of reasons why New Hampshire voters again made a Clinton a "Comeback Kid," but this anger and resentment was one of them. Hillary stormed back, stunning the pollsters, the media, and the Obama campaign and won the primary with a solid majority.

The race was on, and it became one of the closest in history. Hillary and Senator Obama swapped primary victories, and there was a split decision on Super Tuesday, the day when virtually everyone believed that a nominee would be crowned. For the next few weeks there was a series of primaries and caucuses, all of which Senator Obama captured, giving him a lead in delegates and clear momentum. How did this happen?

Because Hillary had gotten terrible advice from her consultants and handlers. They were certain that the race would be over by Super Tuesday, and when that didn't happen, they didn't have the money or the organization to even make it a contest in the five state primaries and four caucuses between Super Tuesday and March 3. Hillary lost them all and was especially crushed in the caucus states, where her campaign was badly outorganized. It looked like game over, and I sadly believed that Pennsylvania's primary would again be rendered meaningless. But it's just not possible to count Hillary out. On March 4 she surprised the experts again by winning both the Ohio and Texas primaries. The delegate race was close again, the Obama momentum had been stopped, and Hillary had now captured almost all of the big states: New York, California, Ohio, Texas, Florida, Michigan, and Massachusetts. Pennsylvania was the last big prize. Hillary had to win it to keep going the momentum she had coming out of Ohio and Texas and to convince the "super" delegates that she was the most electable Democrat in November.

By a quirk in the primary and caucus calendar, there was only one other primary between March 4 and April 22, the date of Pennsylvania's primary, and that was in Mississippi, a state where there was no real contest. Hillary's campaign had conceded it. So the eyes of the nation were riveted on Pennsylvania, and the pressure was intense. Hillary had to win big.

I quickly became deeply involved in the campaign. I helped plan the schedule not only for Hillary, but for Bill and Chelsea, too. The campaign staff listened mostly because Hillary did. Hillary had truly hit her stride, and she was an indefatigable campaigner. For seven weeks we covered the state like a blanket. Hillary spent her time in the most populous cities and suburbs. I decided that we should deploy President Clinton in smaller cities and counties where they had never seen a president. It worked like a charm. For example, I wanted to send him into Carbon County, a small Democratic county that had eleven thousand registered Democrats. I called Keith McCall, the Speaker of the Pennsylvania House of Representatives, who was from Carbon County, and asked him how many people we could get for a late afternoon rally in Jim Thorpe, the county seat. He said three thousand and I said, "We're on!" When the day came, there were three thousand screaming Democrats in front of the county courthouse. If each one had two more voters in their families, the president would have reached nine thousand of the eleven thousand registered primary voters. On Election Day we got 72 percent of the vote in Carbon County. That pattern was replicated everywhere. Senator Obama would come in a few days a week and make two to three stops a day. We would make more than thirty stops a week with a Clinton. I also made sure that we had the support of virtually every elected official in the state.

We had a great closing rally on the eve of the election in Philadelphia, at the Palestra college basketball arena. It drew ten thousand people, and three thousand listened outside. The place was electric! The enthusiasm was contagious and continued over to the next day. Hillary swept the state and won the big victory she needed by a margin of 10 percent.

Our strategy proved to be incredibly effective. The small counties where the president campaigned gave Hillary an average of more than 66 percent of the vote. Hillary lost Philadelphia but held her own in the Philly suburbs and won almost everywhere else. I was on the phone with President Clinton as the returns rolled in and he asked me for the county-by-county vote. When I told him how well she had done in the counties he alone had visited, he asked me to bring the tally to their suite at the hotel. When I got there, he took great delight in showing Hillary that her best vote was in the counties where only he campaigned. She laughed and kidded him back. All three Clintons (Chelsea, too) were elated, and the ballroom where Hillary made her victory speech was going bonkers. We all thought we were listening to the next president.

It was not to be. Even though Hillary won most of the remaining primaries, some by huge margins (West Virginia, Kentucky, Puerto Rico), and wound up getting more popular votes, Senator Obama received the most delegates and the support of most of the "super" delegates. Since Obama went on to win the national election handily, many people may forget that this game went into extra innings and that Hillary lost by only a run. But this was as close as any election gets, and I won't forget that. Perhaps when President Hillary is sworn in in 2017, everyone will be talking about it again.

I said that I fell in love with Hillary during those seven weeks, and I did. It was not just her relentless tenacity or her keen intelligence that made her a quick study, able to simply grasp the most complex issues that bowled me over. It was her sense of humor (especially the ability to laugh at herself) and grace under pressure. In the gossip-fueled best seller *Game Change* the authors said that Hillary was tough on her staff and treated them badly.

Keep in mind that books like that rely on sources, and those sources are usually aides from rival campaigns or disgruntled advisers bitter about not getting a job with the candidate wherever he or she ended up. I spent a lot time working on the Clinton campaign, and none of that happened in Pennsylvania. It was almost exactly the opposite. I was with her and the staff for four or five days a week—at rallies, small meetings, traveling on the campaign plane—and I never saw her treat anyone with anything less than care and sensitivity. Even when someone had screwed up, I saw her sit next to that person on the plane and talk quietly about what happened and how to correct it. Hillary is a great person, and these qualities would make her a great leader for America.

This campaign was good for me. I got a great deal of credit for Hillary's victory—some deserved, some embellished—and a great deal of national publicity. *Time* magazine had an article about me—"Hillary Clinton's Secret Weapon in Pennsylvania"—with a full-page picture. I was on national TV constantly during the seven weeks of the Pennsylvania campaign, and in the weeks following became the TV spokesman for it, so much so that some reporter said I was "the last of the Mohicans." I was proud to be with her until the end, and when we got to the convention in Denver, I was stunned to find how popular I was with Hillary delegates from all over the country.

At each rally we had in the primary campaign, I would introduce Hillary, and before she spoke I would lead the crowd in chanting, "Hillary, Hillary . . ."; I hope I get to do it again.

Hillary has said publicly that she has no interest in running for president in 2016, that she will be too old, and that it's time to let younger Democrats step forward and run. I believe she means it. She is bone-tired—the job of secretary of state is far more grueling than that of the president, with the nonstop traveling, the constant jet lag, and the odd-hours phone calls to accommodate foreign officials' schedules. Still, I believe that when she gets some rest and has a chance to reflect on what she wants, the challenges facing the country will be too great for her to resist and she will change her mind.

I'm already campaigning to persuade her to do so. I have told her that I would be her campaign manager and not even take a salary, that's how important it is for her to run. And her record as one of the best-ever secretaries of state isn't going to hurt her chances.

At a recent dinner where Hillary was honored by the John Marshall Society, I went up to her and asked, "Hillary, do I look like I have the energy and stamina to run for president?" She replied, "Of course you do, you look great." I said, "Well, I'm exactly the age you will be in 2016!" She laughed, and I learned later that when she came to work the next day, she told her staff about our conversation right away.

Run, Hillary, run. This country is so screwed up it needs a brilliant, charismatic, non-wuss lawyer to turn it around!

CHAPTER 19

Change We Can Believe In

How the Best Communicator in Campaign History Has Been Badly Outcommunicated as President

T he year 2008 was dominated by Barack Obama. During the first ten months of the year he made one great speech after another that called America to a higher purpose, to change the way our government operates, to change our national priorities. Each speech created a vision of a new America that touched the emotions of anyone within earshot and so deeply moved them that they did things they had never done before—such as vote! Young people turned out in record numbers. African Americans did as well. Poor, disenfranchised whites found a champion. Reporters violated the rule of neutrality.

Senator Obama's speeches soared. They drew crowds in the tens of thousands. His legend as a communicator grew and grew.

Even when faced with adversity such as the bigoted rantings of his pastor, the Reverend Jeremiah Wright, he came through with the right message. Not a soaring, visionary speech this time, but a thoughtful, quiet explanation of racism in America and his own feelings. It was moving and was hailed by the media as perhaps the greatest speech on race relations ever made.

Fast forward to November 3, 2010. On that night the Democratic Party was massacred, losing more than sixty seats in the House of Representatives, six Senate seats, and scores of governorships and state legislatures. Though there were many reasons for the crushing defeat (the recession, for one), the experts and the media laid the blame mainly at the doorstep of the Obama administration. Though the president remained fairly popular, the policies of his administration were not. This was especially true of two of his most important legislative achievements—the Economic Stimulus Act and the Health Care Reform Act. Neither act was perfect and there were substantive mistakes in both. The procedures the administration followed to get the bills passed were severely flawed. In both cases, the administration deferred to Congress far too much in the drafting of the specific substantive policy. This caused the bills to be Christmas-treed with a great number of things that shouldn't have been included.

But the main reason why these two crucial and vitally needed legislative initiatives were viewed so negatively by the American people on that Election Day (exit polls showed that an astounding 50 percent of Americans wanted the Health Care Reform Act repealed) was that the next Ronald Reagan and his administration had been badly outcommunicated by the Republican spin doctors and their cohorts in the media. How did it happen? What caused this stunning development? How did the best communicator in campaign history lose his touch?

I know how it happened, but for the life of me, I don't know why. The first rule of political messaging is that if you have the "bully pulpit" and you are introducing a new program, take the initiative and explain it first to your constituents as directly and clearly as you can. Define the plan and the issues it presents before anyone else does. The Obama administration never did that with either bill, and as a result the Republicans defined them for the American people.

Let's start with the Economic Stimulus Bill, which was the first major effort by the president. Mistake number one: letting Congress write the specifics of the bill. The administration deferred to Congress, and the well-meaning progressive leadership in the House put in dollars for many social programs that did not create or retain jobs (I am not referring to the education and Medicaid dollars, which I will discuss later). Doing this created two problems for the president. First, it robbed him of the chance to talk about his proposal and its specific initiatives before anyone else did. He lost the chance to define it and spell it out for the American people. Second, it allowed Congress to load up the bill with programs that became easy to ridicule and gave the Republicans talking points to deride it. These programs were a minuscule part of the overall bill but became the face of the economic stimulus legislation. Examples of this were:

- $50 million for NEA grants
- $50 million for farm service computer technology upgrades
- $2 billion for child care subsidies
- $250 million for state grants to create data systems for education and workforce agencies
- $15 billion in student financial aid
- $1 billion for new computer systems for the Social Security Administration
- $225 million for domestic abuse services
- $375 million for victim assistance, child predator tracking, and youth mentoring
- $3 billion for miscellaneous criminal justice services, including community-oriented policing programs
- $200 million for furniture for the Department of Homeland Security

- $165 million for habitat restoration, including fish hatcheries and other wildlife improvement projects
- $146 million for National Park Service trails
- $500 million for wildfire management activities
- $246 million tax break for Hollywood movie producers to buy motion picture film
- $25 million for tribal alcohol and substance abuse reduction

Although I support the goals of an overwhelming number of projects listed above, they had virtually nothing to do with job creation and shouldn't have been in an "economic stimulus bill." Worse still, it allowed the Republicans to deride the bill as having little or nothing to do with job creation by pointing out $50 million for NEA grants; $50 million for farm service computer technology upgrades; $600 million for victim assistance, domestic abuse services, and youth mentoring; $200 million for furniture for the Department of Homeland Security; and $25 million for tribal alcohol and substance abuse reduction. Once they did that, the stimulus program never recovered, and any chance for future stimulus was, in the public's mind, dead in the water.

The second big mistake by the administration was not using its best weapon, the president, to talk directly to the American people to explain the components of the bill and how they would help to revitalize the economy. President Obama did comment on the stimulus program later on a number of occasions, but never with a detailed explanation of what was in the bill and why each part would have a positive impact on the recession.

What should the administration have done? In a way the right answer would have been easy to achieve and extremely effective. The president-elect met with all the nation's governors in Philadelphia on December 1, 2008, less than a month after the election, to get our input on what should be contained in the stimulus legislation. We gave him a lot of advice, some of it good, and they listened to our concerns and incorporated most of this into the legislation. I was chairman of the National Governors'

Association, and I urged members of the Obama transition team to write their own bill. I had some additional ideas that I didn't communicate, and I regret not having done so. Would they have listened? Who knows? But Vice President-elect Biden, whom the president-elect put in charge of the stimulus implementation, is a longtime friend.

Here is what I believe they should have done. First, as I urged, the administration should have written their own tight, focused bill, sent it to Senate Majority Leader Harry Reid and Speaker Nancy Pelosi, and told them to get it enacted. Remember, at this time the president's approval rating was nearly 80 percent, and he had tremendous momentum. Second, they should have told them to pass it before Inauguration Day so that the president could sign it into law within hours of taking the oath of office. Just think about the symbolism. Our new president driving a bill speedily through Congress and signing it into law on Inauguration Day! After that, no one could ever say that the President had ignored the economy.

The night of Inauguration Day is, of course, reserved for balls, but the very next night—Wednesday—they should have had the president address the nation to explain the Economic Stimulus Bill and why each part of it would help the economy:

- Infrastructure spending: explain how this would help meet the country's critical need to revitalize our roads, bridges, water systems, electrical grid, etc., while creating hundreds of thousands of good-paying jobs that couldn't be out-sourced both at the construction sites and in the factories producing the needed steel, concrete, asphalts, etc. Experts believe that every $1 billion of spending on infrastructure creates twenty-five thousand jobs.
- Extension of unemployment benefits and increased food stamp benefits: explain how these additional funds would help stimulate the economy because they are spent more quickly than anything else and are spent at retail stores and other local small businesses.

- Additional funding to the states for education and Medicaid: at first blush these may not seem to have a direct effect on the economy, so there would be a need to explain that they would help the states, which have had huge short-falls in revenue, so they wouldn't have to lay off legions of teachers and other government workers such as police, fire-men, and EMT personnel.
- Tax cuts: The Economic Stimulus Bill called for $375 billion in tax cuts out of the entire $870 billion. This should have been explained loudly and clearly, especially that the cuts were going to families and small businesses. This was the Republican mantra for reviving the economy in early 2009, and the president should have made it clear that the stimulus provided for exactly the tax cuts they had long advocated.

How many Americans know that more than 40 percent of the stimulus spending was for tax cuts? Hardly any, because it was never explained to them clearly at the onset of the legislation. Even worse, how many Americans would say that they received a tax cut from President Obama's stimulus act? If you went into the streets of any American city, stopped the first thousand work-ers who made less than $200,000 annually, and asked them if the Economic Stimulus Act cut their taxes, how many would correctly say yes? Fewer than fifty out of a thousand! Why? In part, again, because it wasn't clearly explained to them. Had the president given this speech in prime time on his second day in office, would it have been different? You betcha it would have.

The administration also erred in the way it implemented the tax cut to working families. It reduced the average worker's pay-roll tax, but it was so little on a weekly basis that few noticed. Had the administration sent each worker a check ($800 if married, $400 if single) at the beginning of the year, no one—*no one*—would have ever forgotten that his or her taxes were cut by the stimulus bill. In fairness to the administration, they were told by economists that a weekly reduction in payroll taxes would free up income that would surely be spent, while a big check would have gone into savings. I'm not sure I agree with that premise, but even if I did, I still would have urged sending the check. It would have had a dramatic effect on public opinion and may have made passage of additional economic stimulus possible down the road.

Almost the very same mistakes were repeated by the administration involving passage of the Health Care Reform Bill. Think about this: in 2008 nearly 70 percent of Americans believed that all American should have health care; virtually all of us believed that we needed to control and reduce the ever-increasing costs of health insurance; and almost all of us believed that the most onerous conditions imposed on consumers by health insurance companies needed to be reformed.

The health care legislation approved by Congress did all three of those things: it expanded access to health care to thirty-one million Americans who had none, and it controlled costs and would bend back the curve of rising health care inflation (though not as much as I would have liked to see). Also, it reformed the insurance industry so it can no longer deny coverage for preexisting conditions; can no longer put a limit on an individual's yearly lifetime expenses; must allow parents to include their children on their policy until they are twenty-six years old; and cannot eliminate someone from coverage if he or she becomes sick.

Yet the legislation is today enormously unpopular. How did this happen? Again, the administration let Congress write the bill, and it was expanded in ways that were unpopular. Again, the president didn't address the nation and spell out the details of the bill until it had been defined by the Republicans. The administration lost control of the messaging from the get-go. Remember the ridiculous, but effective, Republican and media spin about "death squads"? Though it was patently false, it was the only discussion about the health care bill for a couple of months at a time when the administration needed to be controlling the dialogue.

The false information flow wasn't just about "death squads." Most Americans now believe that the Health Care Reform Act will dramatically increase the federal deficit. The truth is that the Congressional Budget Office (CBO) says that in the first decade the legislation will reduce it by nearly $1 trillion. Most Americans believe the bill is bad for senior citizens. The truth is that seniors benefit mightily because the legislation plugs the doughnut hole in their prescription drug coverage ($250 in 2012) and totally eliminates it in five years. Most Americans believe that this bill will increase costs for small businesses. The truth is that it will cut costs starting in 2012, when businesses with fewer than twenty-five employees who provide health care will get a 35 percent federal tax credit to defray those costs, and in 2014, having the insurance companies compete by listing their costs on the exchanges will lower costs for all small businesses.

So again, as with the stimulus bill, the administration lost the communications war with disastrous consequences that played out on Election Day 2010, and the president never got credit for two landmark pieces of legislation that, despite their flaws, greatly benefited the American people.

CHAPTER 20

"Know When to Fold 'Em"

During my eight years as governor I never had a Democratic legislature. I always had to get some Republicans to vote for the progressive legislation I proposed. We never failed to get any of our major initiatives into law, and I was able to achieve substantial progress in every area I had promised during the campaign. Many people would ask me how I was able to do this with a Republican legislature. I always replied, quoting from a great Kenny Rogers song, "You've got to know when to hold 'em, know when to fold 'em." By that I mean you have to know when to compromise and give up some of what you are seeking and know when it's important to dig in, stand your ground, and fight. Or to quote from another song, by the Rolling Stones, "You can't always get what you want!" The key to success is knowing where, when, and for what you have to draw the line in the sand.

The best example occurred during my tenure as governor in my annual fights for increased education funding. As I've touched on earlier, my first budget caused a rancorous battle. Facing a $2.4 billion deficit, I knew I had to raise taxes, but I wanted to get something for that tax increase, so I proposed adding $500 million for early childhood learning. Naturally, the Republicans went crazy and balked at any increased education spending. Neither they nor I, would budge. I knew I had to stand and fight because, first, if I caved in my first year, they would think they could always run over me and, second, because we desperately needed quality pre-K education, full-day kindergarten, and after-school tutoring. There was a five-month stalemate, and finally I knew when to fold 'em on two key issues. First, I compromised on my request for $500 million and agreed to a little less than $300 million. Second, I gave in on making those dollars available to districts that would use them for programs I knew would work. The Republicans supported an idea put forth by their able leader, Sam Smith, and wanted the money to go in an "accountability block grant," which would give districts a far greater number of ways to use the money. They wanted this because of the time-honored (and absurd) tradition of local control of education decisions. I knew from talking to so many district superintendents that they would mostly use the money for the programs we favored. So I could still mostly accomplish our goals and give the Republicans a "victory."

So on December 20, 2003, we had a budget, and this early childhood money started the incredible progress we achieved during my time in office.

The education battle never stopped; we fought nearly every year. It reached a fever pitch in 2009 and 2010 in the teeth of the recession. I agreed to cut virtually every line in our budget, but I insisted on using federal stimulus money to increase education funding. I knew the progress we were making and I wanted to continue it for my entire eight years. The Republicans, of course, wanted to use the stimulus money to reduce spending. I was resolute! We were winning the education battle, our kids were improving faster than any others in the nation, and I wasn't going to stop.

In both years the stalemate went on for what seemed like forever. As I mentioned earlier, in 2009 we finally got a budget on October 9 (the law says we should have one by June 30). I asked for a $300 million increase, and we successfully passed a budget with the additional $300 million. But it proved harder in 2010, when we agreed on a budget on July 6. I asked for $354.8 million and settled for $250 million. ("You can't always get what you want!") Ours was the only state in the Union to give a substantial increase in base K–12 education funding during the recession, and it paid off.

This didn't happen without cost to me. Many state workers didn't get paid during these delays (they were all paid retroactively after we settled), and many services were held up. Initially in 2009 I received most of the blame for the impasse. My favorable ratings plummeted to the low thirties and, déjà vu, I was protested everywhere I went. Then my great media team began to publicize that I was staying in Harrisburg all summer while the legislature, used to adjourning for the summer the first week of July, was nowhere to be found. I canceled a planned August safari to Africa; they went on extended vacation. I even stayed in Harrisburg on weekends sitting by the "pool" at the governor's residence (the pool was a little plastic tub that my goldens, Maggie and Ginger, would soak in). We would invite reporters in to interview me and to take pictures of me and the pooches sitting by the pool (me doing work). It was priceless, and we turned the table in our favor.

The key to this story, though, is that after the struggles, we passed some laws that had bipartisan support. I didn't start this debacle *in order* to win over the public. The point was always getting the right legislation passed. A lot has changed about our politics in the past decade or so, and one is how many government officials forget that. They think they've been elected to make speeches and go on TV and get reelected. The hard part, where you have to find real solutions to real problems, becomes the part they want to avoid.

When I took office as governor, Pennsylvania was not only facing a huge deficit, but we were also in the midst of a serious recession, and our economy was headed in the wrong direction. We ranked forty-sixth among the states in job creation. I had campaigned promising that the first thing I would do upon taking office was to propose an economic stimulus plan. (Back then "stimulus" was not a dirty word.) Shortly after taking office I met with legislative leaders of both parties and outlined for them a $2.3 billion plan that put money into eighteen separate pots (you can still find the details of this plan online at http://www.newpa.com/find-and-apply-for-funding/economic-stimulus-plan/list-of-stimulus-programs). I told them that we would finance it by selling economic development bonds. They initially recoiled from the thought of borrowing that much money until we showed them that Pennsylvania had a very low debt ratio and a great bond rating. After that, they agreed. I let them review the eighteen different initiatives and make suggestions for additions or deletions. That turned out to have real benefits. They made four major suggestions—three good and one bad. The good ones were made by Republican Senate leader Chip Brightbill, Republican representative Steve Nichol, and one by Senate and House Democrats. Senator Brightbill, a really bright guy, knew that nonprofits such as hospitals could not take advantage of the wide array of tax credits our stimulus plan offered, so he developed a program called the Infrastructure Finance Improvement Program (IFIP). This allowed nonprofits as well as for-profits to use the state income tax that would come from the new jobs the project would create in its first ten years to finance a bond to give them up-front construction money. We added it, and this program has become a real success, helping tons of major hospital expansions in the state and many new factories as well.

Representative Nichol's idea improved my venture capital proposal. I wanted our state to become a hub for venture capital investment, so I proposed to allocate $400 million to venture funds that would make investments only in Pennsylvania companies. Representative Nichol said that we didn't need to spend $400 million of the taxpayers' money and that we could accomplish the same goal by setting up a venture guarantee fund that would guarantee the first 50 percent of their investment if the company folded. He was right, so we converted $300 million of the program to venture guarantees and left $100 million in direct investment. Very little of the guarantee fund was ever used, but it had the desired effect of promoting private investment.

The third good idea came from the Democratic caucuses in the legislature, and it involved our proposed "Building in Our Sites" program, which was designed to bring back to life abandoned and polluted sites. Many areas of the state, such as the Pittsburgh region, were losing businesses that wanted to come to their areas but didn't because those areas didn't have any "shovel-ready" sites. So we decided to create a $300 million fund to loan counties and cities funds to clear sites. They would repay the loan from taxes they received once the sites were developed. It was a good plan, but the Democratic legislators reminded me that in some of the state's poorest communities the only way they would get someone to develop the land was to abate the taxes, so there would be no revenue from the site to repay the loan. They were correct, so at their urging we converted the program into part grant and part loan. It turned out to be a godsend for our hardest-hit communities.

The one bad idea came from Republicans' belief that giving the state more than $2 billion to distribute would just allow me to do favors for my wealthy contributors. I didn't do that as mayor, nor would I have done it as governor. I have always given grants and loans based on the merits of the project. (I come from the radical school of governance that believes the way you get reelected is by doing a good job now.) The Republicans didn't believe it—perhaps that tells you something about how they run things themselves—so they created some ungodly entity called the Commonwealth Financing Authority (CFA), and amended the legislation to require all funding from the stimulus to go through it. They gave the governor one vote and each of the four caucuses one vote (Republicans and Democrats in the

Senate and in the House) as well. Funding decisions had to be unanimous, so any one of the caucuses, as well as the governor, could block funding. In their minds this gave them their piece of the pie and a great vehicle from which to gain campaign contributors. It was a terrible idea, opening the door to political chicanery, favoritism, and constant delay, but they made it clear to me that no CFA, no economic stimulus legislation.

I was faced with a tough choice. If I vetoed the bill because the CFA had the potential for real trouble, I would lose the $2.3 billion that I was convinced would jump-start our lagging economy. The policy purist in me badly wanted to veto, but I knew I had to fold 'em and do the practical thing. I had to take the $2.3 billion and hope the CFA wouldn't wreck the initiative. I did and it didn't. It slowed down the needed distribution of those dollars into the economy because of the need to get all five votes, and it often led to all-out bickering, but the money got out and it leveraged $19 billion of private-sector investments. The stimulus was the main reason why Pennsylvania's unemployment rate was lower (sometimes way lower) then the national rate for ninety-three of the ninety-six months when I was governor.

I faced a similar choice when I was district attorney. The US Supreme Court had handed down decisions in the famous *Miranda* and *Mapp* cases that gave defendants enhanced rights affecting confessions and searches and seizures. It meant that a new process of pretrial evidence suppression hearings had to be conducted in almost every felony case, which would require many additional assistant district attorneys.

So I asked the City Council for money to have twenty-five new prosecutors. After the hearing on my request, the Council president, George Schwartz, asked to see me in his office. He told me quite calmly that I could have the needed money if he could pick five of the twenty-five. Every fiber of my body tensed. This was anathema to me. I had prided myself that I had run a DA's office that was totally nonpolitical, and nobody was going to make me hire political hacks. But then my practical side won, and

I folded again. I realized that I desperately needed new prosecutors and I would get to choose twenty good ones. If I stood on principle, we would get nothing and the people we were sworn to protect would suffer. So I said okay, and in a surprise bigger than the Appalachian State upset of Michigan, one of the five, Tom McGarrigle, turned out to be really good (he was actually a law review student). The other four, who were truly the epitome of political hacks, I was able to hide in the child support unit, where they could do little or no harm because they didn't deal with violent offenders; and some of them actually learned and became valuable members of our team.

During my time as mayor I was faced once again with a Hobson's choice. I very much wanted to extend domestic partnership benefits to my workforce. It was unfair that a city worker who had been in a committed relationship for thirty-five years could not extend benefits to his or her partner while a straight worker who had been married for three months could do so. The key benefit was covering the partner with health insurance, enabling real estate transfers between partners, and protecting our lesbian, gay, bisexual, and transgender community from discrimination in employment, housing, and public accommodations.

It seemed to me that this would be easy legislation for the City Council to pass. Virtually all of our major universities and hospitals and most of our big companies (including Disney!) had already given their employees domestic partnership benefits. However, the Catholic Archdiocese of Philadelphia waged a strong campaign against the legislation. Cardinal Anthony J. Bevilacqua asked to see me and told me that the Church loved its gay parishioners and that being gay wasn't a sin, that only having gay sex was a sin. So I asked if the Church expected its gay congregants to be celibate and he replied, "Why, yes!" That conjured up a number of responses in my overactive mind, but for once I held my tongue in check.

Failing to dissuade me from seeking the legislation, the Church ordered every priest in the city to hand out preprinted cards addressed to me and the City Council, denouncing the concept. The priests were required to talk about this during their sermons and urge their parishioners to send in the cards. I got forty-four thousand but was unmoved and didn't wuss out because of an overflowing mailbox. But the Council, not so much. They buckled and sent my great friend Council president John Street to ask that I not force them to face either the wrath of the Church or the disappointment of the growing political clout of the city's LGBT community.

Again I was on the horns of a dilemma. I very much believed in domestic partnership benefits, and I wanted to win this for our gay community, with which I had forged a great relationship during the previous sixteen years. It was fair and the right thing to do.

But I had already pressured the Council to make a number of tough, courageous votes against city unions when the galleries were packed with screaming city workers. Again, knowing when to fold 'em, David Cohen and I decided to withdraw the bill and grant city workers those benefits by executive order. I could legally do so for all benefits except pension rights, which could only be vested by statute. I knew that a few years later, when the climate improved, legislation would pass granting those, too. It did.

So by folding, I was able to preserve my great relationship with the Council. Together we went on to take many difficult stands, to draw that line in the sand, to hold out for the change that helped to turn Philadelphia around and get the city back on its feet.

This was one of my proudest achievements—turning around a legislative body that before I became mayor could be swayed by ten people with signs, a legislative body that gave the word "wuss" a bad name into a tough, strong group. The City Council truly became a "no-wuss zone."

CHAPTER 21

Please, Please Don't Honor Me

The minute you get elected to any important governmental job, people want to start bestowing honors on you. I could never figure out why. What for? I haven't done anything yet! I may turn out to be a horrible mayor, I might make a mess of things. Why not wait until I actually do something?

The most striking example was President Obama being given the Nobel Peace Prize in 2009. What? Come again? He had been in office for nine months, was presiding over two wars (one of which he intensified—in Afghanistan), and had authorized increased use of killer drones. A little ridiculous? Even Obama recognized that, saying it was less for his accomplishments and more "a call to action."

This wasn't President Obama's fault. He said in his acceptance speech that he didn't deserve to be on a list with other great winners but that he hoped his actions as president would support the prize in retrospect. It was, of course, the fault of the five-member Norwegian Nobel Committee, and the person who nominated him just days after he took office. What were they thinking?

The Nobel Committee is not alone by any means. Every organization seems compelled to honor you no matter how long you've been in office or what you've accomplished. Most do it with the dreaded plaque. During my time as DA, mayor, and governor I have received thousands of plaques. You can't stop the flow, you can't discourage the organizations from giving them to you. When I was mayor we would store these plaques in a back room in alphabetical order so that if any of the members of a given organization were coming into the mayor's office to see me we would quickly retrieve the appropriate plaque from storage and put it up on a wall!

There is *nothing* you can do to stop the flow of plaques. When I became mayor of Philadelphia I instructed my head scheduler to send letters asking groups not to give us a plaque, but to give us a donation of whatever they would have paid for the plaque to the Recreation Department or the Free Library. We sent them out to everyone, but almost no one listened. I arrived to find no check, but always the dreaded plaque!

By the way, the most important person on a governor or mayor's staff, with the possible exception of the chief of staff, is the head scheduler. That person must have great patience, great people skills, a keen mind, and an infinite capacity for abuse. I have been very lucky to have had great schedulers—Karen Lewis, Susan Siegel, Eden Kratchman, Phyllis Halpern, Nolan Reichl, Alex Ficken, Sarah Battisti, Betsy Phillips, and Kaylan Dorsch (you can tell there is a fast burnout rate!).

The plaques got bigger, more flowery, and more grandiose in my last years in office as mayor and governor. The verbal tributes were head-turning. Your last year in office you go to events or to see groups whose events you have attended each and every year, but they treat you like retiring pro athlete on his farewell tour.

One group honored me with a plaque stating that I was the best mayor of the century. When I got up to speak I thanked them for the honor but asked "How can we be sure I was the best in this century? None of us was around in 1910, 1916, 1920, etc. And conversely, why did you stop at century? Why not the best mayor of all time? Ben Franklin was never mayor." For a moment the crowd was speechless. Then I broke into a big smile and they knew I was kidding. Nonetheless, as long as there are elected officials, there will be plaques. In fact, plaque production may be one of the few recession-proof industries.

I have a firm belief that politicians—even we courageous non-wusses—should never have anything named after us while we are still alive and surely not while we're still in office. It's embarrassing to say the least, and it can lead to some even depressing consequences. Consider the sports arena built as part of the Meadowlands complex in the 1970s in New Jersey. Brendan Byrne was governor of New Jersey, and a very good one, whose initiative helped the complex get built. So they named it after him. Okay, that's nice; I would be mortified, but different strokes, I guess. Well, Governor Byrne has had a long and fruitful life, which is, of course, a great thing, except that he has lived long enough to see his name unceremoniously removed from the arena as it was renamed the Continental Airlines Arena. Of course, Continental, which hubs out of Newark Liberty International Airport, paid big bucks for the honor. Brendan helped create it, but money trumps gratitude. *Sic transit gloria!*

I have done a good job enforcing my belief when it comes to myself. I have let a few scholarships be named after me, but no inanimate buildings or objects (no Edward G. Rendell bridges—whew!). There is one exception, however: the "Edward G. Rendell Tree," or, more accurately a dreaded plaque in my honor placed at the base of a tree. How did it happen? What caused me to deviate from my firm belief and create an exception? My neighbors did.

I have lived for more than thirty years in a great little section of Philadelphia called East Falls. It's got blue-collar families and professionals, gays and straights, old and young, rich and not so rich. In our midst are two of the best private schools in the nation, Penn Charter and Germantown Friends, and Philadelphia University, an excellent local college. Our neighborhood is beautiful, friendly (carolers still go house to house), and full of spirit and pride. I could live virtually anywhere, but I can't conceive of ever leaving the Falls.

Well, a group of my neighbors came to me as my time as mayor was coming to a close and said they wanted to honor me as the first mayor to have lived in East Falls by naming something in East Falls after me. I told them of my strict rule against such things. They were undeterred and said we want to do it in McMichael Park. I was aghast. Morton McMichael had been mayor, too, from 1866 to 1869, and I had visions of the Brendan Byrne Arena saga (McMichael was dead, but I was sure he still had family in the area). They said not to worry, that they had no plans to name the park after me. (I confess I was a little deflated—surely I was a better mayor than McMichael, and he didn't even live in the Falls.) They wanted to honor me by placing a plaque at the base of a big oak tree in the middle of the park. They were so enthusiastic and so earnest that, against my better judgment, I acquiesced.

The big day for the naming ceremony arrived. The plaque was truly beautiful, a rich bronze with a wonderful message expressing the pride the neighborhood had in me. The ceremony was very nice, about seventy people were there, and I was truly touched. I began to wonder if I should reconsider my naming ban. But about a month later I had an experience that quelled any change in policy.

My two rescue golden retrievers, Ginger and Mandy (I know their names sound like two strippers), and I would go for walks on the campus of Philadelphia University, several blocks away from McMichael Park. But on this day I decided to check out my plaque and we took a leisurely stroll up to the park. As we got to the edge of the park I saw something very strange and very unexpected—there was a queue of dogs at my tree. As we drew closer it became clear that this lineup was all male dogs and they were waiting to relieve themselves on my plaque. Apparently one dog did so shortly after the dedication ceremony, and his scent was so strong it compelled all the male dogs of East Falls to beeline to it so they, too, could leave their mark. It was sort of amazing to watch the queue's uncanny accuracy. My beautiful plaque had turned from that rich bronze to a sickly yellow in just four weeks. I couldn't decide who had suffered a more humiliating fate—Brendan Byrne or myself—but you can be sure that my no-naming ban is back firmly in place!!

CHAPTER 22

Build, Baby, Build

"Infrastructure," the Least Sexy Word in the English Language

There is no greater example of the wussification of America than the growing neglect of our nation's infrastructure. Talk to a young man today, and he'll marvel at the way his father's and grandfathers' generations knew how to make and fix things. That's not just for oil changes and water heaters; that goes for bridges and roads, too. When we were a young nation we were imbued with that pioneer spirit—we would try to accomplish anything, no matter how daunting a challenge, if it was necessary to grow our country or expand our economy. The roadblocks in front of us never scared us, never caused us to back down, and never impeded our progress.

We built the Erie Canal over an eight-year period, and when we did, it opened up commerce between the Atlantic coast and the Midwest. It was a key step to our building a national economy, and it set off an explosive period of growth. At the time, building the canal was a monumental challenge, from an engineering standpoint and from a fiscal one as well. But those challenges didn't deter us. Sure, there were naysayers, who called it too big and too expensive. But we also had leadership back then who understood that it takes bold decisions to create a better future.

When Lincoln said we needed to construct a transcontinental railroad, we simply did it. The same positive reaction was given to Ike's plan to build a national interstate highway system. We did it in short order, and it helped to make us the number-one economy in the world. When Ike left office in 1961, the United States was spending roughly 10 percent of its nonmilitary domestic spending on its infrastructure. Today that has fallen to 3.5 to 4 percent, we no longer have the world's best infrastructure, and we are heading to becoming a second-rate economic power.

I have always been focused on the needs of our infrastructure. In 1998 I succeeded Mayor Bob Lanier of Houston as head of Rebuild America. In 2001, after I left as chair (naturally), Rebuild went out of business. After I became governor I wanted to bring Rebuild back to life, and I looked for elected officials to join me as co-chair. I also knew that for our new organization to succeed it had to be more than just Democrats. So I looked for co-chairs who, first, had taken action on infrastructure, and second, were not Democrats! I found that Arnold Schwarzenegger, the Republican governor of California, had drafted and helped pass a $42 billion referendum that called for investment in the Golden State's infrastructure. Similarly, the mayor of New York, Michael Bloomberg (then a Democrat turned Republican, but now an actual independent), had devoted more resources to fixing and revitalizing New York City's infrastructure than any US mayor in history. I wanted them to join me, and on January 2008 Building America's Future was born. It's been an extremely worthy successor to Rebuild America and has established great credibility in Washington and with the media as the leading voice for infrastructure revitalization in the nation. Our superb staff, led by Marcia Hale and

Kerry O'Hare, released a report called "Falling Apart, Falling Behind," which highlighted the disastrous state of our infrastructure and how it is causing us to lose ground in the global economy. For example, in 2005 the World Economic Forum ranked us as having the best infrastructure in the world, but just this year, in their latest evaluation we came in fifteenth. What's worse is that we are rated as having the eighteenth-best rail system, the twenty-second-best port infrastructure, and, unbelievably, the thirty-second-best air transport infrastructure, behind nations such as Panama, Malaysia, and Chile.

What a disaster! How did it happen? Why did we let it happen? What should we do?

The magnitude of this disaster is hard to imagine and even harder to believe, but consider the facts. The American Society of Civil Engineers issues a report every five years on the state of our infrastructure, and in 2009 they gave it a D, with our bridges getting a C and our roads getting a D-. More shockingly, they said that we had a $2.2 trillion infrastructure deficit, meaning that we would have to spend that much just to bring our infrastructure — our roads, bridges, water and wastewater systems, our school buildings, our dams and levees, our ports and airports, our electrical grid and broadband, and our air traffic control system — up to just *fair* condition. If you think this is an anomaly, consider that the National Surface Transportation Policy and Revenue Study Commission, formed by our Congress in 2005, found that we need to be spending $160 billion a year more on just our transportation infrastructure alone to put it in passable condition. (Current spending in the United States — federal, state, local and private — is $84 billion a year on it. The committee recommended upping it to $224 billion a year.) The United States now has 4 million miles of roads and 600,000 bridges, and, according to the US EPA, we must invest $334.8 billion over the next 20 years to provide us with enough safe water.

It's hard to believe that we have let our infrastructure decay to such condition, given its importance to us in so many areas.

First, our public safety is at risk by a "falling apart" infrastructure. That's true whether it's the bridge that collapsed in Minneapolis, the levees that gave way in New Orleans and Cedar Rapids, the pipeline that burst in Santa Monica, the steam pipe that blew up in New York City, or the closing of I-95 in Philadelphia. All of us are at risk everywhere across the land. My good friend Terry O'Sullivan, head of the International Laborers' Union, felt so strongly about this that in four states he paid to have billboards put up at the beginning of bridges that read, "The bridge you are about to cross is structurally deficient. Call Congressman Jones 202-757-4359!" That got people's attention, but I wish Terry had done what he told me he had thought about doing—placing a second billboard at the end of the bridge, saying, "Glad you made it!" That would have swept the country! Terry told me his lawyers talked him out of it. Damn lawyers! They are the master practitioners of "wusscraft"!

All Americans care about their safety and that of their families. Second, the state of infrastructure significantly impacts our quality of life. Congestion wastes a massive amount of time, fuel, and money. According to the Texas Transportation Institute's 2010 Urban Mobility Report, in 2009 Americans stuck in traffic wasted 4.8 billion hours and 3.9 billion gallons of fuel for a total congestion cost of $115 billion. The same report also said that the yearly peak period delay for the average commuter was thirty-four hours in 2010—up from fourteen hours in 1982.

In August of my last year as governor, Chris Christie, the governor of New Jersey, and I announced that Pennsylvania and New Jersey would collaborate on a public-private partnership that would widen and substantially improve the Scudder Falls Bridge, on which I-95 passes over the Delaware River. During rush hour the traffic jams are incredible, and it is estimated that these improvements could cut the delay time of a commuter who goes over the bridge twice daily by nearly an hour a day. If that proved to be true that would give the commuter back 5 hours a week and 250 hours a year—that's more than 10 days of their lives back.

Ten days to play with their kids, to pursue their hobbies, to play golf, to talk to their spouse—you get the picture.

Americans want that time back. They want the improvements in their quality of life that a first-class infrastructure can buy.

Third, polls and focus groups conducted by Building America's Future have found conclusively that Americans understand that a better infrastructure can keep us economically ahead of our competitor nations. It's something they want very badly, but as our infrastructure falls behind that of other countries, we are in danger of becoming a second-rate economic power.

For example, the ability to move goods quickly affects a company's bottom line. Delays and inadequate facilities add to US companies' costs. Take the condition of our ports. I already told you our port infrastructure is ranked twenty-second-best in the world, but absorb this fact: of the ten ports that have the most throughput today, none is American and six are Chinese. Worse yet is the fact that in 2012 the port of Shanghai will be able to process more cargo than the ten largest US ports combined. To give you a graphic example, let's look at the case of metallurgical coal. It's a type of coal found mostly in the United States and Australia. It is an essential ingredient for the production of coke, which is vital to the steel industry. China is in great need of coke and, therefore, seeks to buy as much metallurgical coal as possible. Labor costs in the United States and Australia are roughly the same, but because Australia has a better transportation network, the coal there can reach their ports for about a fourth of the cost that it takes in the United States. Thus we lose a great deal of China's business to Australia.

To illustrate the point further, consider the following from Building America's Future's "Falling Apart and Falling Behind" report:

Delays in freight movement impose real costs on businesses that reduce productivity, impede our competitiveness, and increase prices for consumers. General Mills

estimates that every one mile per hour reduction in average speed of its trucking shipments below posted speed
limits adds $2 million in higher annual costs. According
to UPS, if congestion causes each UPS delivery driver to
incur 5 minutes of delay, it would cost the company $100
million.

Fourth, the biggest issue facing America today is the need
for jobs, and the best answer for job creation is to build back
our infrastructure. Experts, including the US Department of
Transportation, say that $1 billion of infrastructure spending
create 25,000 new jobs. Pennsylvania received $1 billion from
President Obama's stimulus plan to fix our bridges, roads, and
highways. We decided to closely track the number of jobs that
spending would create both at the construction site and back at the
factories that produce the steel, asphalt, concrete, aggregate, and
other materials used in repair or building the bridges and roads.
Not surprisingly, we found that our $1 billion in spending had
created 26,654 jobs. The construction and manufacturing sectors
have been the most hard hit during this recent recession, and best
of all, job in these sectors are well-paying and family-sustaining.
They are also almost impossible to outsource.

Yes, Americans most definitely want good jobs created.

Last, an efficient, well-planned infrastructure can improve
our environment. If we build a more effective, faster freight rail
network, if we eliminate or reduce most traffic jams with thousands of idling cars and trucks, if we develop a more advanced
air traffic control system that will reduce tarmac time for most
planes—if we do all of this and more, we will significantly reduce
the amount of pollution we put into our air.

Consider the following from a report by the American
Association of State Highway and Transportation Officials:

According to the American Society of Mechanical
Engineers, 2.5 million fewer tons of carbon dioxide would

be emitted into the air annually if 10% of the intercity freight now moving by highway were shifted to rail. In 2000, railroads moved a ton of freight an average of 396 miles per gallon. If 10% of the freight moved by highway were diverted to rail, the nation could save as much as 200 million gallons of fuel annually. [http://www.camsys. com/pubs/FreightRailReport.pdf; Freight Rail Bottom Line Report, American Association of State Highway and Transportation Officials, p. 29]

Next, consider air traffic control. In the FAA's NextGen Implementation Plan (the FAA's plan for improving our airport infrastructure, particularly communications), the agency estimates that if the NextGen plan is carried out, we would save about 1.4 billion gallons of aviation fuel, reducing carbon dioxide emissions by 14 million tons between 2010 and 2018.

All Americans want a cleaner, safer environment.

If all Americans want the enhanced public safety, the improved quality of life, the increased economic competitiveness, the additional jobs, and the better environment that a good infrastructure can produce, then how did we, the people let it decay and begin to fall apart?

It happened because we simply stopped investing in, maintaining, and improving it. I related above the decline in the percentage of nonmandatory domestic spending devoted to infrastructure from Ike's time to the present (roughly 10 percent to 3.5 to 4 percent). As of 2011, Canada spends 4 percent of its GDP on transportation investment and maintenance, and China spends 9 percent. The United States spends only 1.7 percent.

To put it simply: if you bought a house, but decided you weren't going to spend enough to adequately maintain it, your house would slowly but surely fall apart. If your roof sprung a leak and you decided not to pay to fix it, the water would severely damage your floors. If you stopped paying for adequate heating, your pipes would freeze, and so on and so on. That's how our failure to maintain our infrastructure has caused it to erode and begin to fall apart.

Why has it come to this? Why have we let this happen? The answer lies with our elected officials. First, because they have made the allocation of infrastructure spending political. The funds aren't distributed where they're needed, where they'll get the best return for the investment. They have been, in great part, allocated by who has the most powerful congressman or senator. Hence we have the Big Dig or the "Bridge to Nowhere." This lack of accountability and transparency has eroded the public's confidence in infrastructure spending (the polls show quite emphatically, however, that the public supports increased spending if it is based on merit, on sound cost-benefit analysis). Second, my friend Mika Brzezinski, the co-anchor of *Morning Joe*, says that "infrastructure" is the least sexy word in the English language. By that she means that it's hard to get people riled up about infrastructure. People understand it is important, but it takes a backseat to what are perceived as more immediate and pressing needs. It is easy to say that we'll get to that next year.

Third, and by far the most important reason, is that it's all the fault of wuss politicians and a man named Grover. The latter is Grover Norquist, perhaps the most powerful man in America (a point he's never been known to argue). Grover, the founder and president of Americans for Tax Reform, has terrified our Congress (and many or our governors and state legislatures) into signing a no-tax pledge, promising that they will *never*, under any circumstances vote to raise taxes or any other revenue. A total of 243 of our US representatives (a substantial majority) and 41 of our senators (enough to filibuster and stop any legislation) have signed the pledge. Most of them know how ridiculous it is, but they must not have thought hard about the consequences before signing it. Either they didn't realize how hard it is to govern without raising taxes, or they thought they could get away with hypocrisy. Now that they've signed this pledge, they are too afraid to do what they know is right. It got so bad that when the federal gas tax expired in the fall of 2011, the Republicans in the House of Representatives went to Grover to get his permission to reauthorize it at the very same rate. Good grief! They needed his promise that he wouldn't construe the reauthorization at the same rate to be a tax increase and, thereby, a violation of their pledge. Aaaaagh! A bunch of pathetic, hopeless wusses.

I was on a Sunday TV show in January 2010, and the moderator asked me to comment on a tape he played for me. The tape showed Congressman Mike Pence, who was then the ranking member of the House Budget Committee, speaking at the conservative C-Cap Convention. He was pounding the podium and almost shouting, "Yes, we're the party of no! We say no to taxes! We say no to spending! We say no to borrowing!" The moderator asked me to comment on what he said and I replied, "That's a prescription for disaster for our country. If we follow that advice, we'll be a second-rate economic power in no time. There isn't a business in America that has grown successful without investing in its own growth, and we have to as well." Fox News, never one to shy away from controversy, invited me and Congressman Pence to appear together the following Sunday. He went first and gave the same riff. Then my turn came and I said, "Congressman, you seem like a reasonable man to me." (In truth he didn't, but I've been on enough TV talk shows to know you want to be the "nice guy.") "Can you tell people watching us how we are going to keep our roads and bridges, our dams and levees, our pipelines safe if we don't invest in maintaining them?" Congressman Pence, who is at least a very smart guy, seemed stunned. He took a little time and then responded, "There you Democrats go again using the word 'invest' when you really mean 'spend.'" Of course, that didn't answer my question, and the truth is there is no answer. We must invest, and we should do it now, when construction costs are low and so are interest rates, which is important if we borrow money to finance some of the necessary work.

Infrastructure repair is like the old 1980s Fram oil filter com- mercial where the mechanic holds up a Fram filter (a few bucks) and says, "You can pay me now or pay *him* later" (showing a mechanic with an engine totally torn apart). It's not going to get any cheaper. And investing in repair can avoid the costs that can come from a collapse. The Army Corps of Engineers had asked for less than $1 billion to repair the levees in New Orleans. It was never funded, and then Katrina hit and the federal government has paid more than $16 billion to repair the destruction.

We can afford to do this. Building America's Future has rec- ommended spending $200 billion a year for the next ten years in additional spending on our infrastructure to enable us to have a well-thought-out, effectively designed, long-term plan to revitalize our country. The Congressional Budget Office found in a 2008 study that $185 billion a year in funding would be offset by the additional tax revenue it would generate and all the direct and indirect benefits that would flow from it. And $200 billion of addi- tional infrastructure spending would produce five million jobs each year for ten years (25,000 x 200). This additional investment would be from combined federal, state, city, and private sources.

The simple truth is that we can't afford not to do it. Wusses, get some backbone, or get out of the way!

Note to wusses: The American people are ready to give you a permission slip to spend money on our infrastructure. They approved 64 percent of the ballot referenda on transportation infrastructure in 2010, during arguably the most anti-spending election mood in any of our lifetimes. Each ballot issue called for increased spending—tolling, taxes, or borrowing. Los Angeles County approved an increase in its sales tax for an infrastructure fund. Charleston, South Carolina, voters did the same, as did Houston, Texas, voters.

And the voters' permission is a helluva lot more important than Grover Norquist's!

CHAPTER 23

Stand and Defend

There Are Some Things Worth Losing For

T here are a few basic truths about politics that I have learned in my thirty-three-year career. The two most important ones relate to governing and its relationship with campaigns. I believe that these truths are self-evident and that politicians of all stripes should understand and heed them. They will allow them to be more effective when governing and to enjoy governing more, and they will increase their chances of getting reelected.

Truth no.1: *There are some things worth losing for.* This is absolutely true. If you, as an elected official, don't believe that, you should resign immediately. In fact, you never should have run for office in the first place. If you don't believe this, you should be forced to answer this question: "Are you here only to do whatever you must to keep your job?"

The truth about point number one is that too many of our elected officials are simply afraid. They are true wusses, and they simply won't take risks if it means potentially losing their job. President John F. Kennedy wrote a famous book titled *Profiles in Courage*, which describes politicians who knew that there were some things worth losing for and took risks to achieve them. In most cases taking these risks, in fact, did cause them to lose their job, but what they did risk for was something they believed in, and it changed our country for the better.

One of the politicians JFK described was John Quincy Adams, the sixth president of the United States. Although Adams eventually rose to the presidency, his initial foray into politics, as a senator from Massachusetts, was short-lived. Adams was a member of the Federalist Party when he became a senator, but his decisions and actions during his term ostracized him from his party. The critical juncture in the souring of this relationship occurred in 1806, when the British began to seize American ships, confiscate their cargoes, and compel our seamen to serve in the king's navy. Although many New England Federalists downplayed the actions of the British, Adams spearheaded the passage of a number of resolutions condemning British actions and requesting that the president demand restoration of and indemnification for the confiscated vessels. Then in 1807, in response to further British aggression, President Jefferson called upon Congress to enact an embargo in retaliation against the British that would essentially shut off all further international trade with them. Although the embargo clearly would have a devastating effect on Massachusetts as the leading commercial state in the nation, Adams was appointed chairman of the committee that drafted the bill and was instrumental in its eventual passage into law. He did this with knowledge of the consequences and he once stated to a colleague, "This measure will cost you and me our seats, but private interest must not be put in opposition to public good."

Not surprisingly, his home state and the Federalists in particular chastised Adams severely as commerce in Massachusetts screeched to an unprecedented halt due to the embargo. In a legislative session after the embargo took effect, the Republican governor of Massachusetts made it known that the session's principal object was the "political and even the personal destruction of John Quincy Adams." The legislature immediately elected Adams' successor nine months before his term was to end. Realizing that he had only one feasible option, Adams resigned in defense of the policies of the very same man who had driven his father from the presidency. Upon his resignation Adams wrote, "[I] am far from regretting any one of those acts for which I have suffered, I would do them over again, were they now to be done, at the hazard of ten times as much slander, unpopularity, and displacement."

Another politician whom JFK described in *Profiles in Courage* was Edmund G. Ross, an obscure senator from Kansas. Ross served as senator during the post–Civil War era, a time when many Republicans sought to treat the southern states as conquered rebels. President Andrew Johnson had become increasingly wary of the radical Republicans, and he decided to suspend Secretary of War Edwin M. Stanton, whom he viewed as a tool of the radical Republicans, and replace him with General Grant. Johnson's actions incensed the radical Republicans, as Stanton's removal was in deliberate defiance of the Tenure-of-Office Act, which prevented the president from unilaterally removing certain officeholders (including Stanton). In response, the House quickly adopted a resolution to impeach Johnson, with every single Republican voting in support of the resolution.

The stage for impeachment was set, and Johnson's impeachment trial in the Senate began. Over the course of the trial proceedings, it became abundantly clear that the Republicans did not intend to give the president a fair trial. Ross continuously expressed concern over the fairness of the trial, and the Republicans began to fear that his support of impeachment was in jeopardy. The Republicans needed thirty-six of their forty-two incumbents to vote for impeachment to ensure Johnson's removal from office. To their surprise, six of the Republican senators indicated that that they did not believe there was sufficient evidence to convict the president via impeachment. It slowly became apparent that the vote of Ross, the only senator who had not committed to conviction with the remaining thirty-six, was the key vote needed to convict Johnson. The Republicans were shocked and outraged that Ross, a strong supporter of the radical Republican agenda, would even consider voting against conviction. In the days and months leading up to the vote, Republicans from across the country feverishly pressured Ross to vote for conviction. Ross, in response to a letter he received from a group of citizens from Kansas, wrote, "I do not recognize your right to demand that I vote either for or against conviction. I have taken an oath to do impartial justice according to the Constitution and laws, and trust that I shall have the courage to vote according to the dictates of my judgment and for the highest good of the country."

As the vote approached, the Republicans still held out hope that Ross would come to his senses and vote with them. On the day of the vote, as expected, only Ross's vote was needed to convict Johnson, and when Ross was called upon to vote, the room was filled with a deafening silence. When Ross prepared to address the room, he stated that he felt that his "powers of hearing and seeing seemed developed in an abnormal degree." In that instant Ross came to realize the magnitude of his decision, and as he later described it, "I almost literally looked down into my open grave. Friendships, position, fortune, everything that makes life desirable to an ambitious man were about to be swept away by the breath of my mouth, perhaps forever." Despite these grave consequences, Ross defiantly stated "not guilty," and with that the attempt to convict President Johnson by impeachment was lost. Although Ross disliked Johnson and opposed his policies, he was unwilling to support what he felt was a trial marked by insufficient proof and partisan considerations. Neither Ross nor any Republican who had voted to acquit Johnson was ever reelected to the Senate, and Ross had indeed thrown himself willingly into his political grave.

I believe that President Obama, like Adams and Ross, has demonstrated these qualities most importantly in his determination to get a health care bill passed, and I believe history will judge him kindly because of this. Many political pundits opine that the president made mistakes in pushing health care reform too quickly. They say he should have focused on the economy first. They also criticize him for going for a large, sweeping bill. They say he should have tried to do it incrementally by phasing it in, seeking passage of the law's popular insurance reforms first.

These criticisms were probably correct from a political standpoint, but I believe the president rejected them for a very important reason that took great political courage on his part. It's my view that he felt deeply that extending health care coverage to thirty-one million Americans was something worth losing for, and he correctly assessed that he had to do it in his first two years, when he was certain to have solid Democratic majorities in both the Senate and the House.

He was right on both scores. It is a flat-out disgrace that the United States is the only developed country in the world that doesn't guarantee health care for all its citizens. And his evaluation of the political chances of passing such an expansion was also dead-on.

The president also showed courage at a critical time in our nation's history. He did the right thing even though he knew it would be very unpopular. First, he continued President Bush and Secretary Paulson's bailout of the financial services industry. The people hated it and the president could have scored big political points by ending it. He didn't, and by not doing so he saved the country, and maybe the world, from virtually complete economic collapse and a massive depression.

He also acted against popular opinion when he bailed out the auto industry. Again people hated it, and many opinion-makers and elected officials criticized him (e.g., Governor Romney), saying that he should just let them go bankrupt and fail. The president knew how important the auto industry was to so much of our manufacturing sector, so he didn't let it fail. For example, in Pennsylvania we don't have any car manufacturing plants, but we manufacture many of the components that are used to produce automobiles. If Detroit failed, so would all of them.

Of course, unlike the financial services bailout, the auto bailout has worked dramatically, and it will be a real plus for the president's reelection campaign. The car companies have paid back a high percentage of their loans, and the American auto industry has come roaring back, using innovation and new technology to produce more vehicles and create many new well-paying jobs.

On balance, in his first term, President Obama has shown great courage in both domestic policy and foreign affairs (e.g., Libya and the raid that resulted in the death of Osama bin Laden). The president is definitely not a wuss, and all three hundred million of us are better off because of that.

However, there was one occasion where the president clearly wussed out, and that occurred in his State of the Union speech in 2011. A few weeks before he delivered it there was a terrible shooting in Arizona, where a crazed gunman killed six people and injured thirteen, including Congresswoman Gabrielle Giffords. The gunman fired more than twenty shots, using magazine clips that held thirty-three bullets. These clips were illegal to make, distribute, or possess under the federal assault weapons ban that, in an incredible act of cowardice, Congress let expire in 2004.

The nation was outraged. The president went to Arizona and made a great speech. He invited some family members of the victims who had been killed (including the family of a nine-year-old girl who had come to hear Congresswoman Giffords speak) to sit in the first lady's box. He also invited Daniel Hernandez,

Congresswoman Giffords' intern whose courageous actions after she was shot probably saved her life.

They sat there during the speech, the media pointed them out, but the president never mentioned them, unlike the others who had been invited to the box. Worse still, he never even talked about the need to enact two reasonable gun control measures that had been proposed and, given the nation's concern over this shooting, might have had a chance of passage if the president had acted when the issue was so ripe.

Senator Frank Lautenberg and Representative Carolyn McCarthy were working to pass their bill to restrict the sale of high-capacity magazine clips, those that hold eleven or more bullets. Their effort was aimed at exactly the type of gun used to mow down the crowd in Tucson.

The other measure that was gathering steam was a push for federal legislation to make sure the background system successfully keeps mentally ill and drug-addicted individuals from legally purchasing a gun. The fact that Jared Laughner was able to purchase a gun was evidence that the national background check system rules aren't working. States are required to report mentally ill and dangerously drug-addicted individuals to the federal gun background check system. Although required by federal law, most states don't make these reports to the federal system, often because doing so requires state legislation to permit these records to be shared at the federal level, or because of lack of funding to handle the workload. The president had a golden opportunity to support the efforts of the law enforcement community by proposing measures to force and promote state compliance with the already in-place federal gun background system requirements. If Arizona was compliant, maybe Laughner wouldn't have been able to purchase a gun.

To me it showed a lack of courage that the White House decided to be silent on both measures in spite of the fact that the tragedy was so fresh in the public's mind. Both enjoyed clear majority support in public opinion polls, but the president never talked about either in his address. It was as if anything having to do with gun control—even this heartbreaking incident—was too radioactive to even mention. I believe that had he recognized his guests and called for the swift passage of both bills the president would have looked like a strong, courageous leader and would have actually gained support. Alas, the White House didn't see it that way.

I believe that in my career I have always been willing to take those risks. I have described a number of those in these pages: indicting the officers who beat Delbert Africa, taking on unions as mayor, appearing with Farrakhan, proposing and passing the second-biggest tax increase in Pennsylvania's history to increase education funding, and strongly advocating gun control in an NRA-dominated state. I can't deny that taking these risks didn't scare me. It sure as heck did, but I decided that I had worked long and hard to get elected as DA, mayor, and governor—in each case an uphill battle against the odds—and wasn't going to wuss out. I was dedicated to fighting to achieve the things I believed in, the things that could measurably improve the quality of people's lives. I was lucky that I took these risks and never suffered from them. I also got reelected and by wide margins. Maybe I did because I was a risk-taker, because people knew I believed there were things worth losing for. All I know for sure is it made the twenty-four years I served in office exhilarating, uplifting, and a whole lot of fun.

Truth no. 2 (the lesson of 2010): *If you run away from what you believe in, you will soon be unemployed.*

In the elections of 2010 there were a number of factors that led to the Democrats' near-historic losses. Certainly, first and foremost among them was the recession. When things are bad, when people have lost their job, lost their 401(k)s, lost their homes, they tend to be pissed off. They also tend to take out their ire on the people in office. That is a tide that it is almost impossible to turn back. A second factor was the extremely successful job of spin the Republicans had done to convince the voting public that the

Democrats had spent their way to a record deficit when in fact it was the Bush administration's policies and the recession that were the main contributors to the deficit. Last on this list was Obamacare. By the time the November 2010 election rolled around it was not either overwhelmingly popular or unpopular, but again the Republicans continued to inaccurately spin it. The truth was, as I detailed earlier, by the time of the 2010 elections the only parts of the Affordable Care Act that had become law were very popular with the public. For example, seniors receiving a $250 check to help plug the doughnut hole in their Medicare Part D prescription drug coverage, or children under twenty-five years of age assured of coverage because they can no longer be denied because of a preexisting condition, or insurance providers being required to give coverage to children up to age twenty-six on their parents' policy.

Notwithstanding, the most moderate ("Blue Dog") Democrats who had voted for the health care bill decided to try to make voters forget that they did so. Fat chance! Many Republican challengers could not be considered rocket scientists, but they weren't that dumb. By running from their vote, the Blue Dogs helped feed the spin that it was bad legislation. Trying to make voters forget they voted for the bill was the stupidest idea since Al Gore's consultants put forth the theory that not having Bill Clinton campaign for him would make people forget that Gore was his vice president.

What these Democrats should have done was stand and defend. Polls consistently showed that voters liked many of the component parts of the health care bill—and they were the parts that had gone into effect by 2010. They should have taken the issue head-on, talked about the good things that had become law and the fact that it's disgraceful that the richest country in the world has nearly 50 million people without health care (again something that polls show most Americans found abhorrent).

And while they were at it, they should have made an issue of the fact that our deficit reductions were not a result of "shared sacrifice" but rather fell almost exclusively on working-class Americans because Republicans refused to let the Bush tax cuts expire for Americans earning more than $250,000 (once again, a tax increase a solid majority of voters polled supported). In short, we didn't campaign as Democrats, we tried to be Republican-lite. Given that choice, voters understandably will opt for real Republicans. We lost so badly because we ran away from the things we have always stood for, from the base values we have always believed in. We didn't fight for what we believed, we didn't stand and defend, and, as a result, many of us were soon unemployed!

CHAPTER 24

"The Charge of the Wuss Brigade!"

As I said earlier, a significant number of our legislators are petrified to even contemplate raising taxes no matter what the money would go for. "Wusses" is too hard a word for them. Most of them find themselves in the dilemma because, during their campaigns, they idiotically signed the Grover Norquist "no tax" pledge, locking themselves into an untenable position. To violate the pledge would bring about swift political retribution from Grover and his minions.

But sometimes the need for additional revenue is inescapable. What does the wuss brigade do? They do intellectual gymnastics that defy reason or logic to avoid raising taxes, and when they do, they raise only "sin taxes"—on cigarettes, liquor, and gambling. Though Grover has never given a permission slip for them to do so, only a small percentage of voters partake in "sin," and polls show that these sin taxes are popular with the rest of us. Thus it doesn't take a profile in courage to vote to raise them.

The five governors of Pennsylvania who preceded me all promised the citizens of the state that they would give them relief from their high property taxes. They all failed because the legislature did not want to raise another tax to offset the revenue that would be lost from cutting property taxes. Today Pennsylvania receives nearly $1.3 billion more in annual revenue than it did before I became governor, and almost all of it goes to property tax relief. As a result, nearly two hundred thousand senior property owners have seen their school property taxes eliminated and almost three hundred thousand have seen them reduced by 50 percent or more.

How did I succeed where the others failed? Simple: "Money for nothing"—I gave them an easy vote. I proposed expanded gaming for our state and introduced legislation legalizing slot machines at thirteen venues. It passed, with many of the "no tax" pledge legislators providing the necessary votes. We did it right, enacting a high gaming tax rate, and as a result, Pennsylvania nets the most revenue from gaming of any state in the nation—more than Nevada and New Jersey. In my seventh year we expanded to include table games, and the expansion passed by an even wider margin than slot machines had.

Gaming wasn't my first experience with the "money for nothing" phenomenon. The slots legislation passed in 2005, but during my first year as governor we were faced with a medical malpractice insurance crisis. In 2002 and 2003 medical malpractice insurance rates spiked by as much as 80 percent and 100 percent. Doctors were threatening to leave the state and were telling their patients that unless Harrisburg did something about it, they would be gone. The people panicked, so I began working on a plan as governor-elect. The plan had a number of components, but the key was "MCARE abatement." In our state, in addition to private coverage from insurance providers, doctors were required to purchase excess coverage from a state-run MCARE fund. For the four specialties that had seen the greatest increases—orthopedics, neurosurgery, obstetrics and gynecology, and general surgery— doctors would, in some parts of the state, have to pay MCARE $80,000 or more a year in addition to the premiums they paid to their private insurer. So I proposed creating a fund to cover 100 percent of the payments for doctors in the four specialties and 50 percent for all other physicians. It was a great idea (which when enacted immediately stopped any loss of doctors and helped alleviate the costs), but, of course, we needed to come up with the revenue. I proposed a 2.5 percent surcharge on the premiums charged by the Blues (Blue Cross and Blue Shield health care plans), which, because they are technically nonprofits, pay virtually no state taxes. The Blues objected fiercely, and their lobbyists spread throughout the Capitol like locusts.

So our legislators were being asked to do two very difficult things: raise taxes (a surcharge is a tax unless you are the one proposing it) and stand up to the lobbyists and special interests. Those wusses folded like accordions. But they realized they had to do something. They couldn't be responsible for doctors leaving the state and leaving the voters, too. So they came up with a brilliant idea—a "sin tax," though this time those evil cigarettes were the target. To produce enough revenue for my MCARE fund they raised the cigarette tax 25 cents a pack. It was "no harm, no foul!"

The most ludicrous example of this "no tax" mania came as a result of another good program we initiated. I believed that renewable and alternative energy development was crucial to our achieving energy independence, protecting our environment, and creating "green jobs" for our economy.

In 2004 we had passed an aggressive law mandating that nearly 20 percent of the electricity produced by our utilities had to come from alternative and renewable energy sources such as wind, solar, hydro, and geothermal. This began a movement toward our goal, but by 2007, I believed we needed to do more. So we proposed an $850 million bond issue to create a fund as an incentive to businesses and consumers to develop and use renewable energy. Again it was a very popular idea, but the issue was how to fund it. We proposed another surcharge, this time to citizens' electricity bills, which for the average homeowner would increase his or her bill by less than $6 per year. No one would have even noticed such a small monthly surcharge, which would have been the cost of one cup of coffee at a convenience store a month. It couldn't have been easier to vote for. Wrong! By 2007 the legislature had become far more conservative, far more ideological, and they considered this to be a tax increase. As happened with the MCARE abatement, Republicans, especially those from southeastern Pennsylvania, did not want to be responsible for killing what became known as the "green jobs" fund. As a result, they performed some stupendous legislative gymnastics. Our state had almost ten years before capped electricity generating rates when we deregulated. Those rate caps were scheduled to come off starting in 2010, and when rates went up, as they surely would, the tax on public utilities would go up as well, and the Republicans pledged that increased tax yield to pay the debt service on the bond issue.

Incredible! Think of the idiotic result that followed from another case of antitax wussiness. Pennsylvania would spend hundreds of millions of its tax revenue—money that could go to education or health care—to avoid a 45-cents-per-month surcharge on an electric bill, even though most citizens polled said they were okay with the surcharge.

In the end, the fund has been extremely successful. The Pew Center for the States found that from 2000 to 2010, Pennsylvania had created the third-highest number of "green" jobs, behind only Texas and California.

If Tennyson were alive today, he might well have written that we are watching "The charge of the Wuss Brigade!"

CHAPTER 25

Does Government Create Jobs?

P oliticians always debate whether government actually creates jobs. Most of them say "no"; they say that the private
sector and only the private sector creates jobs. The Republicans,
especially, pay constant homage to the "job creators." If I hear
that we can't raise taxes on the "job creators" one more time, I'll
barf. If raising taxes on the "job creators" will kill job growth, how
do they explain the 1990s? In 1993 Bill Clinton raised taxes on
the top 2 percent of Americans—the fabled "job creators"—and
in the next 7 1/2 years there were 23 1/2 million new jobs created in America. Raising taxes and eradicating the deficit may not
have caused that job growth, but it sure didn't "kill job growth" or
"throw us into a recession," as the conservatives warned in 1993.

In fact, in the past sixty years the highest marginal federal
income tax rate stood at 70 percent during the five years in which

we experienced our strongest job growth and at 35 percent or below during the four years of our lowest job growth. In fact, in our twenty best years of job growth, only one year was at the highest marginal rate of 35 percent or below. Case closed!

If you have hung with me this far, you are not surprised by that at all. Can government actually create jobs? Sure it can. FDR created millions of new jobs with the Civilian Conservation Corps program. He put people to work in cities, in our national parks, on our highways, and so on. When Ike decided that we were going to build an interstate highway system that would be the envy of the world and provided federal money to make it happen, he was surely creating millions of construction and manufacturing jobs. When Bill Clinton created Americorps he was creating hundreds of thousands of jobs for young people. So the question is not whether government can create jobs, it's whether doing so is a good thing. In most cases, absent a deep recession, the answer is no.

Government can and should invest in our nation's growth. As detailed earlier, if we invested in a ten-year infrastructure-revitalization program, spending an additional $200 billion per year, we would help create five million new jobs in the private sector each year. These would be well-paying jobs that couldn't be outsourced, and people would be put to work doing something that the country vitally needs—rebuilding bridges, roads, dams, levees, and water systems and expanding our electrical grid and broadband capacity.

Government should also invest in energy to help our nation achieve energy independence. Doing so would create millions of jobs. Finally, additional government investment in medical and technological research would be a surefire way to create new jobs and drive our economy. Just imagine the number of jobs if our research led us to create a drug that cured cancer. This would create a significant number of jobs for production and distribution. It would be sought after throughout the entire world. All of these jobs—in infrastructure, energy, and research—would be in the private sector, fueled by government investment.

More than anything, government should create the conditions and the environment best for job growth. There are basically four things that government can and should do to create the environment necessary to promote growth. First, it can ensure the existence of a ready supply of workers trained to fill the jobs that industry wants to create and the jobs that require a new level of technological skill. That task starts with improving our K–12 educational system. When I was running for governor in 2002 I toured the Sony TV production plant in Westmoreland County, southeast of Pittsburgh. After the obligatory photo ops of me with a white coat and special glasses looking at giant TVs, I asked the Sony execs how I could help if I became governor. The didn't ask me for the usual grants or incentives, but said I should do everything I could to improve K–12 education, because in the ten years they had been in Pennsylvania they had seen the skill set of high school graduates (66 percent of their workforce were high school graduates who trained themselves on the job) deteriorate dramatically. That experience was one of the reasons why I was so adamant about improving education.

Government has the added responsibility of providing job training in the areas in which the private sector is hiring and to train in fields in which there is a real anticipation of growth. So, for example, in Pennsylvania a Lehigh County school district worked with UPS and set up a replica of a UPS packaging and shipping operation at the school. UPS then hired the kids who had successfully navigated the training program. A good example of training for anticipated growth is the emphasis that both the federal government and many of the states have put on training for jobs in energy conservation.

This is smart policy because it has become clear that we will never be able to produce enough energy to meet the exploding world demand, so conservation is a must. In fact, several states, including Pennsylvania, have enacted aggressive conservation mandates. So it is essential that workers be trained to do everything from retrofitting buildings to installing smart meters that control energy use.

Government can aid job growth by helping business's bottom line. That is especially true today in the competitive global marketplace. That means lowering tax burdens, unemployment and workman's comp costs, and health care costs. The last one is especially important because in most cases American businesses are competing against companies who pay no health care costs at all because their countries have universal health care. The Affordable Care Act is a step in the right direction. In Pennsylvania we were much more aggressive in cracking down on and controlling the costs of hospital-acquired infections; treating chronic conditions such as diabetes, asthma, and heart and lung disease; and lowering emergency room costs by expanding the scope of practice of nondoctor medical personnel such as certified nurse practitioners, pharmacists, and physician assistants.

The third way by which government can aid businesses and thereby assist in job creation is by having a sensible, workable, and predictable regulatory program. I am all for adequate regulations to help ensure our health and safety, but in promulgating and applying them we must use common sense and consistency. They must be enforced in a way that doesn't impede growth. For example, when building a bridge or constructing a highway it is important to do an environmental impact statement or an environmental assessment. But often these reviews take one to two years to finish. Nonsense! There is absolutely no reason why they couldn't be completed in six months. It's amazing what we can get done when we are pushed by appropriate time limits.

Last is the question of incentives, what some people call subsidies. I believe that government can and must help the private sector create jobs by giving incentives when necessary. This is especially true when we know that our competitor nations, especially China, do it all the time. A great example of this type of appropriate incentive is the research and development tax credit. The credit, often both state and federal, can free up corporate bottom-line dollars so they can do more R & D that will hopefully lead to new areas of enterprise that create those important new job opportunities in cutting-edge science and technology.

So can government create jobs? Yes, it can, but it's best at formulating public/private partnerships that allow the "job creators" to start creating.

CHAPTER 26

Is Honesty the Best Policy?

Often in my thirty-three-year political career, I have gotten in trouble for things I have said. This occurs, in great part, because I have always answered every question I get asked honestly and bluntly. Although this caused me trouble in the short run, it has been one of my strengths in my long-run popularity. A perfect example was my response on the night the US Supreme Court decided *Bush v. Gore*. As I detailed earlier, it got me in hot water with the Gores, the DNC staff, and almost the entire Democratic establishment, but people sided with me and almost universally believed that I said the right thing.

A second reason why I have gotten into trouble for my responses is that I frequently don't stop and weigh the consequences of what I am saying. My media director for my last six years as governor, Dr. Kirstin Snow, would stand in the back during my many press conferences and shake her head. She was clearly thinking about how she and our press office would try to clean up the damage I invariably created at almost every one.

A perfect example of this occurred at a press conference when I was expressing my frustration at the Republicans in the legislature who were against spending money no matter how good the program was or how effective it was in reaching its goal. I said that these guys are so bad they wouldn't raise taxes if it would cure cancer the next day. All hell broke loose, but you know what? That statement was dead-on about a number of Republicans in Harrisburg, and sadly, it's proving to be equally true about a large percentage of Republicans in Washington, DC. (If this cure is great, you can hear them saying, the free market would already have created it!)

As mayor, I got into trouble with my own Jewish community not just because of my Farrakhan appearance but because one night when I was receiving an award from a Jewish organization, I wanted to say something that was more than just the usual awardee's thank you and stock response. So I took the opportunity to talk about my experience as a Jew. I started off by relating how when I was five years old my father took me and my brother aside and told us that he and our mother had decided not to raise us in the formal Jewish religious traditions. We weren't going to attend synagogue or be bar mitzvahed. He explained his reasoning to us by saying that he had found that many Jews in his industry (the garment district of New York City) who spent the longest time in shul on Saturdays were the biggest crooks from Monday to Friday. He went on to remind us that he wanted us never to forget that we were Jews, to remember the struggles of the Jewish people, and to help Jewish causes as much as we could.

I related all of this and even told the audience that I remember the Six-Day War in 1967 as a young twenty-three-year-old, and hearing that Israel was losing in the first days and that, even though it would have no bearing on my life, I was rooting as hard as I ever have for them to prevail. Yes, even though I didn't attend synagogue and never was bar mitzvahed, I understood I was part of something larger: I was a Jew and proud to be one. I started to tear up as I related all of this, and many in the audience did the same. Despite that, the next day the *Jewish Exponent* only reported that I called many Jews who go to synagogue religiously "crooks." Good grief!

As governor my verbiage seemed to get me in more and more trouble. Perhaps it was because I was receiving a whole lot more coverage. The election of 2008 began my rocky relationship with the Obama staff, caused by my honesty and quirky sense of humor. Of course, in the Pennsylvania primary I was for Hillary, and early on I predicted that from my experience running for election in our state there were some parts of it where voters simply wouldn't vote for an African American candidate. That was absolutely true, of course. For example, when I ran for reelection in 2006 a number of voters in our rural areas said they were voting for me not because I was a great governor but because they wouldn't vote for a "black guy."

Again, though, this comment caused a furor. Tony Norman, an African American columnist for the *Pittsburgh Post Gazette*, wrote a scathing column. He wrote:

> I know I have a habit of sometimes zoning out in these meetings, but it sounded to me like Mr. Rendell had unilaterally declared Pennsylvania to be Alabama circa 1963. Was he suggesting that Pennsylvanians are uniquely racist in ways that folks in the states Mr. Obama has won so far aren't? By the way, Mr. Obama won Alabama on Super Tuesday, thank you very much!

Interestingly, when he reflected on the entirety of what I said, he wrote what was essentially a retraction:

> Thanks to an item in my column on Tuesday, Mr. Rendell has had to deal with a tsunami of unwanted and unflattering national attention. The column was picked up by political Web sites and quickly metastasized.

If the hundreds of e-mails and dozens of calls I've received since Tuesday are any indication, the governor is being unfairly pilloried as a crypto-racist provocateur for suggesting that there are whites in this state who aren't ready to vote for a black candidate — i.e., Barack Obama.

Those of us who live in this state are painfully aware that there are many parts of Pennsylvania that will never be confused with a racial Shangri-la.

Notwithstanding this, my statement caused a furor.

After the primary and Hillary's withdrawal, there was some speculation that I would be a great vice-presidential running mate for Senator Obama. The theory was that I would help bring over the angry Hillary supporters and, of course, Pennsylvania was crucial for a Democratic victory. In truth, there was never a chance I would be picked, for who in their right mind would want an uncontrollable free spirit such as me as a running mate, or worse still, as their vice president?

But whatever infinitesimal chance there was went up in smoke when I was asked on TV about my prospects. I quipped, "Well, we would be a truly balanced ticket – Senator Obama doesn't wear a flag pin, but I do!" Seconds after the interview I got a call from David Axelrod, the senator's brilliant media guru, ripping me — and my dreams of living in the Naval Observatory and attending countless funerals went up in smoke. I told David that the campaign needed to get a sense of humor or they would never make it to November. They never did get a sense of humor, but they made it to November just fine.

Since President Obama took office I have been critical of the administration's performance on a few occasions but mostly a steadfast supporter. But I stepped in it again during the controversy over the administration's handling of BP's oil spill in the Gulf of Mexico. I was making the point that their substantive response had been right on target in every way, but that the president hadn't been visible enough down in the Gulf region and that that had created some of the negative feedback. I went on to contrast the president's activities to what President Clinton, a master of the hands-on response, would have done. Not only would he have been in the Gulf region, but also he would have been in the Gulf in a wet suit, trying to plug the leak personally. Shockingly, the White House didn't see the humor in that either. I got a raft of criticism for that as well. The president's staff thought I was public enemy number one. They totally ignored the countless times I appeared on TV supporting the president and attacking his critics. But one night I got lucky. I was on an MSNBC prime-time show and the first two speakers were progressives who bashed the president for turning his back on the base of the party. Then the host introduced me and said, "And let's hear from Governor Ed Rendell, President Obama's staunchest defender." I was in seventh heaven. As soon as the show ended I directed Donna Cooper, my policy secretary, to get the transcript and send it to every key White House staffer with the words "staunchest defender" highlighted.

Sometimes I say things that are truthful and blunt that I later regret because they are also hurtful. The class of 2002 newly elected Democratic governors had a great number of superstars, and chief among them was Janet Napolitano, a former prosecutor who had been elected governor of Arizona. She is smart, focused, a great leader, and very funny. We hit it off from our first meeting and loved to swap stories about our political brethren. I was at a Democratic governors' event in Phoenix and I read in the paper that the Republican Speaker of the Arizona House had said that full-day kindergarten had no positive benefits. The next day at a press conference Janet was asked about his statement and I jumped in and said that had to be about the stupidest thing I had ever heard any elected official say. Janet was delighted because I delivered the message and she could stay above the fray. I was thrilled that virtually nobody in Arizona had ever heard of me, so it was a freebie for me.

But a few years later I unintentionally hurt my good friend by being careless and thoughtless. It was December 1, 2008, and President Obama asked all fifty governors to come to Philadelphia to talk about what should be in his stimulus proposal. I was chairman of the National Governors' Association at the time, so I headed up the meeting. Needless to say, the national media were all over the meeting, and there were microphones in front of the head table where I sat with the president-elect, the vice president-elect, and Governor Douglas of Vermont, the NGA vice chair. The meeting ended and I mistakenly assumed the mics were dead. Governor Douglas asked me what I thought about Governor Napolitano being named by the president-elect to be the secretary of homeland security. I said right into a live microphone, "Perfect for that job. Because for that job, you have to have no life. Janet has no family. Perfect. She can devote, literally, nineteen to twenty hours a day to it." What I meant was that protecting us from terror threats is a round-the-clock, no-vacation job. I would have said the same thing about myself. At that time my son was thirty years old and married, and my wife and I both worked nonstop at our jobs.

I meant no offense to my very good friend. But many commentators inferred it to be an insult to women who weren't married, and my remarks were characterized as antifeminist. One commentator, from CNN, acknowledged on the air that I am a "good guy" but really ripped into me. I assumed that this spin made my remarks hurtful to Janet and I was depressed, not about the bad publicity I might have received but because I might have hurt or embarrassed a good friend. But Janet came though like a champ and said that not only was she not offended, but also that she knew exactly what I meant and understood it. This made me love her even more and it made me resolve to think before I speak (a resolution that probably lasted three or four days).

CHAPTER 27

The Top Ten Reasons Why Most American Politicians Are Wusses

Ever since David Letterman debuted the first Top Ten list, I have been enamored with the concept and have composed them for birthday parties, farewell parties, anniversary galas, office parties, and so on. So I couldn't write a book without including at least one. Here goes:

10. They Refuse to Give Credit to a Rival No Matter What He Does

The crowning example of this was Republicans' criticism of President Obama's handling of Libya. By any objective standard the president's approach to Libya was a huge success. The people of Benghazi escaped genocide, not a single American life was lost, and the brutal dictator Gadhafi was deposed at a cost of less than a thousandth of the price of the Iraq War. Nevertheless, the Republicans just couldn't bring themselves to give him credit. First, they criticized him for waiting too long before acting. Then when he did act, they pounced. Senate Republican leader Mitch McConnell wondered, "When this operation will end and when our loved ones will return . . . what is the mission?" And finally, when the mission ended in complete success, they praised NATO, the British—good God, even the French—anyone but Obama. Nothing but toady wusses!

9. They Refuse to Admit Mistakes

This is a common trait of many elected officials. It's wussing out and it's bad politics, too. There are many examples, most notably Mayor Michael Belandic, whose Chicago administration botched removal of a nineteen-inch snowfall. The mayor denied that they had screwed up and blamed it on the sheer amount of snow. It didn't wash, and on this issue he was defeated in a primary election by Jane Byrne. Politics 101: If you or your people screw up, stand up, admit it, and say that it sure as hell won't happen again. Think of what might have happened if the incredibly talented Anthony Weiner, insistent on denying at first that the pictures were of him and concocting a story that his website had been hacked, had admitted the truth from the get-go, apologized, recognized he had a problem, and said he was going to get help. He might well still be in Congress had he done so. If you blow it, don't be a wuss; confess it and take your medicine.

8. They Refuse to Answer
Questions from the Media

Ronald Reagan was a wuss (only in part) because he consistently ducked questions from the media by feigning that he couldn't hear them when he walked to his helicopter or by terminating his press conferences prematurely. Many other elected officials just hole up and refuse to have press conferences, or if they do, they only make announcements and refuse to answer any questions. No elected official who deals with the media over any length of time actually likes doing it, but if you believe in democracy, you are honor-bound to do it. The media are your main way of communicating with your constituents, and they have the right to see or hear you answer tough questions and defend what you are doing.

7. They Don't Have the Courage to Say No Their Base

Elected officials are so scared of losing, they simply will never go against the wishes of their base, their core group of supporters. We have discussed their reluctance to stand up to the NRA on even the most absurd issues, such as the previously discussed one-gun-a-month legislation. Another case is Republicans' throwing red meat to their base by attacking Planned Parenthood funding under the guise of being prolife and antiabortion when they know that federal law already bars Planned Parenthood from getting any money for abortion counseling and that their funding is already restricted to family planning and women's health activities.

Our side is no better. We can never seem to stand up, for example, to the teachers' unions. Everyone knows that our educational system needs more accountability for principal and teacher performance. In each one of my eight years as governor I called on the legislature to enact new rules requiring accountability and got virtually no Democratic support. If it were a secret ballot, 80 percent would have been for the reforms. Come on, people. It's okay to disagree with your friends every once in a while.

6. They Refuse to Debate

When a politician is running for election and has a big lead there is a tendency not to debate his or her opponent, to chicken out and not give the opponent a chance to close the gap. LBJ, leading

Goldwater by 36 points, said no, as did Richard Nixon, leading Hubert Humphrey by 10 points and George McGovern by 25. The tough-talking Republican congressional leaders Darrell Issa and Eric Cantor also wussed out on debates in 2010, saying they were "too busy at work," but Cantor was not too busy to go on a book tour promoting his book *Young Guns*.

Sometimes the strategy of ducking debates works; sometimes it doesn't (in 1968, Nixon didn't debate and saw his big lead over Humphrey shrink to 0.7 percent on Election Day). But regardless of the political calculation, it is wussiness personified. Democratic commentator Paul Begala said it best: "There are few potentially unscripted moments in a campaign and I think people ought to know . . . if the candidate can't handle a single interaction with the opponent, how are they going to handle the pressures of office?" Paul's dead right. Debates are at the heart of the democratic process, and candidates have a duty to participate. When I ran for reelection as mayor and governor I received 80 percent and 61 percent of the vote, respectively, but I debated because I respected the process. By the way, Governor Rick Perry of Texas refused to debate his challenger Bill White when he was seeking reelection in 2010. After watching him in the 2011 presidential primary debates, we can understand why!

5. They Refuse to Stand by Their Votes

To me, there is little worse than an incumbent running for reelection who tries to hide from votes he or she has cast. I have already discussed the prime example of this: Democrats in 2010 who voted for health care reform trying to hide that fact from the voters. Or Democrats or Republicans who voted for the financial services and auto industry bailouts and then tried to push that fact under the rug rather than defending them as votes that were hard but drastically necessary and that turned out to be successful in averting full-fledged disaster. There also were many Democrats who did gymnastics to avoid taking responsibility for voting to authorize the Iraq War ("I was against it before I was for it").

4. They Refuse to Speak in Front of Protesters

A real profile in wussiness? Tough-talking Eric Cantor was scheduled to give a speech at the Wharton School in Philadelphia on
October 21, 2011. He pulled out and refused to come after discov-
ering that the speech, on income inequality, was to be open to the
public and that protesters from Occupy Philadelphia, the AFL-
CIO, and MoveOn.org were planning to attend. The school
denied that his speech was ever to be closed to the public. But
what difference does it make? A skilled public speaker can almost
always turn the presence of unruly protesters to his advantage,
making them look bad and himself look good. And come on,
Eric, you bill yourself as a "young gun"; you can handle the
Occupy guys. Or should your book be retitled *Young Wusses*? But
Eric is not alone. Politicians of both parties routinely back out
when protesters arrive. Many Democrats and Republicans fled in
August 2009 when Tea Party members arrived to protest health
care reform. The best example of courage under fire that summer
came from Senator Arlen Specter, who faced down Tea Party protesters at one of his own town meetings. He looked tough, courageous, and the epitome of a non-wuss.

3. They Change Their Positions as Early and as Often as You Change Your Socks

Egad, you could write a book about how politicians change positions to curry favor with the voters. I do believe that when you are
confronted with changed facts it is okay to change your position
on an issue. So if you voted to authorize the Iraq War because you
believed that Saddam really did have weapons of mass destruction
and then, when time revealed that there was no evidence that he
had any, you could then legitimately change your position and be
against the war.

But when there is no material change in facts and your position shift is for purely political reasons, that is wussiness of the first degree. For example, Mitt Romney on abortion and gun control. Or Newt Gingrich saying that the Ryan budget was "radical right-wing social engineering" and then, faced with conservative criticism, the very next day saying that he "erred." What convinced Newt that he made a mistake? What new fact did he learn? Or did he change because of criticism from Rush Limbaugh, Charles Krauthammer, and others? Take a bow, Newt, you are an all-star wuss!

2. They Run from Their Allies at the First Hint of Trouble

See how they run. Many people in politics have the loyalty of a snake. Actually, that's probably unfair to snakes. When things are going well for you in politics, other elected officials want to be seen with you, want your help, want their picture with you, and so on. But if you fall out of favor, you might feel like you have developed leprosy.

A case in point: A former governor of Maryland, Parris Glendening, who had used President Clinton's help in the past, snubbed him twice after the Monica Lewinsky scandal broke and refused to appear with him. Then when it became clear that President Clinton had retained his popularity, the governor asked him to come to Maryland to do a fund-raiser for him. This was, even for politicians, a completely amazing transmogrification (a College Board word) of the governor's position.

President Obama, whom virtually everybody adored in 2008, is going through some similar experiences in 2012. He carried the city of Detroit in 2008 with 74 percent of the vote, and yet when he appeared there in mid-2011 not a single member of the state's congressional delegation showed up. Simply amazing. Give those wusses the red badge of courage. Even worse, Senator Claire McCaskill, who was a key Obama supporter in 2008 because she legitimized women not being for Hillary, didn't show up in 2011 when the president took his jobs pitch to St. Louis, where he was also doing a fund-raiser. She remained in DC, explaining on Twitter that if she went with the president she would have been criticized for "hobnobbing with big donors." Come on, Claire, you have been a great senator and usually displayed limitless courage. You're too smart to think that by staying away from the president people will forget you were a strong supporter!

1. They Take Credit for Things They Voted Against

Nothing is worse, nothing is more hypocritical, and yes, nothing is wussier than a politician voting against a program and then turning around and attending a ribbon cutting of a project it funded, acting like he or she was responsible for the program becoming law or, alternatively, asking for money from the program for projects in the district.

The ultimate example of this happened after passage of the heavily criticized stimulus bill. Not one Republican in the House and only three in the Senate voted for the stimulus, and almost all of them reviled it, scorned it, and savaged it. Nevertheless, that didn't stop them from asking for money from it or attending ribbon cuttings that followed its implementation. A total of 128 Republican congressmen did just that, including some big names:

The holier-than-thou Paul Ryan (WI), who had called the stimulus "a wasteful spending spree" that "misses the mark on all counts," wrote Secretary of Labor Hilda Solis for a grant from the stimulus so a group in his district could "place a thousand workers in green energy jobs." Another hypocrite, "young gun" Eric Cantor (VA), ripped the bill and then asked for money from it for high-speed rail in his district. Presidential candidate and anti-government spending Ron Paul (TX) nevertheless asked for $3 billion for NASA from the bill. Kevin McCarthy (CA), a House leader, sent out a release taking credit for getting money for a new federal courthouse—"we worked together for years to overcome many obstacles"—but never mentioned that the money came from the stimulus. Steve Scalise (LA) did the same thing, taking credit for getting a COPS grant (money to buy police technology equipment), again without mentioning that the funds came from the stimulus program. Tim Johnson (IL) and Bob Shuster (PA) both attended groundbreakings for grants for an intermodal transportation facility and a sewage treatment plant, respectively, taking credit for stimulus-funded projects.

Good grief! What chutzpah!

The same thing happened to me when as governor I proposed spending $220 million to put laptops on the desks of every high school in the state and give teachers a smart board and training on how to use this technology to teach. It revolutionized high school in our state. The students caught fire and paid rapt attention. Solving problems on computers was challenging, but fun and rewarding, too. The students, teachers, and parents all fell in love with the program, called "Classrooms for the Future," and so did Republican legislators, almost none of whom voted to support it, and almost all of whom denounced it as "wasteful spending." Notwithstanding this, they would visit the "classrooms for the future," taking credit for the program. I bet that the words "Governor Rendell" were never uttered once during any of those visits. In fact, a Republican state representative sponsored a bill proclaiming "Classrooms for the Future Day," and it passed unanimously. Guess whose name didn't appear once in the proclamation lauding the great state program. Ah, I'm a prophet without honor, even in my home state!

CHAPTER 28

How to Get Our Democracy Back on Track—Electoral Reform

T he American democracy, the best system known to man, is
in trouble. Our country has become great by always adapt-
ing to face new challenges as they arose, but our election system
today is desperately in need of reform in three very important areas.

1. The Primary and Caucus System

Our nominating process is a hybrid. A great deal of its process is
under the control of the political parties. So, for example, in 2008
Republican rules permitted winner-take-all primaries, whereas
Democratic rules divided delegates by the percentage of the vote
each candidate received.

For an example of the chaos that can stem from party control, look no further than this year's Iowa caucus. Three weeks after the caucus, the Iowa Republican Party still had not certified a winner. First, they said Governor Romney won, then that it was a tie, then that Senator Santorum won, then they gave up and said they simply didn't know; and finally they said that it was Senator Santorum.

Given that the systems are controlled by the parties, it is difficult to mandate change, but change is sorely needed. The caucus system is truly unfair and undemocratic. Because you have to be present to hear presentations by the candidates' representatives to be able to cast a vote, it has the effect of disenfranchising seniors who may be physically unable to come out, single parents who can't get a sitter, and anyone who works the 4 to 12 shift. There are also no absentee ballots, which only further limits who can cast votes.

First, the system should be changed to mandate all primaries or that if the caucuses are to remain, the process should be changed to allow some form of absentee voting.

Second, the calendar must be changed. There is no reason why Iowa and New Hampshire should always go first and, thereby, have a disproportionate impact on the nomination. In 2008 had Barrack Obama followed his win in Iowa with a victory in New Hampshire, it would have ended the race. The nomination would have been decided before any big-city dwellers had cast a vote, and before Latinos and African Americans had a chance to make their voices heard.

The reason given for preserving the current system is that there is an advantage to making the candidates do retail campaigning and it allows candidates with less money a chance to win and gain momentum. Well, those rationales are flawed. In this year's Republican contest Rick Santorum, a poorly funded candidate, spent an inordinate amount of time in Iowa doing multiple town meetings in every one of the state's 99 counties. It paid off, and he finished in a surprising dead heat with front-runner Mitt Romney. But because the New Hampshire primary was so close—one week later—Santorum didn't have time to use his great showing to build any momentum or raise any money, and he finished in a poor tie for fourth in the Granite State.

The amount of retail campaigning in these two states is absurd. Candidates spend well over a year meeting their voters, while in states like New York, Georgia, Illinois, Missouri, and California, they campaign among the voters for often less than a week. This absurdity was best depicted by a cartoon in the *New Yorker* in 1988 when there were seven candidates vying for votes in the New Hampshire Democratic Party primary. The cartoon showed a lady at her front door talking to Governor Dukakis and telling him, "I'm sorry, Governor, there is nothing you can do for us now, Senator Gore is mowing our lawn and Congressman Gephardt is doing our wash!"

The best way to cure this defect is to adopt a plan offered by the National Association of Secretaries of States in 2000 and have five regional primaries consisting of ten states each one month apart. They would be held on the first week of the month starting in February and going through June. Every presidential year the regional primaries would move so each would have a chance to be first every five elections.

The critics of this plan say it would favor well-funded candidates, but I'll address that a little later.

2. The Electoral College

We desperately need to amend the Constitution to do away with the Electoral College and replace it with the popular vote.

Four times in our nation's history a president has taken office despite the fact that more Americans voted for his opponent (that's four out of fifty-six presidential elections). That's unfair, undemocratic, and tragic. However, it's not the worst thing that could happen under the electoral college system. If there was a legitimate third-party candidate with significant appeal who carried four or five states and, as a result, neither of the two major party candidates received the 270 electoral votes needed to win, the election of the President of the United States would be made by the sitting House of Representatives. That would be a true fiasco and a real stain on our democracy.

The defenders of the Electoral College system say that it's the only way any attention is paid to the small states because in a straight popular vote system no one would campaign in the Idahos, Delawares, and Rhode Islands. That may be true, but in the majority of small states (for that matter the majority of all states) no one campaigns in them now. States that are solidly red or solidly blue get virtually no attention. Having participated in eight presidential elections, including one as Democratic Party Chairman, I can tell you that presidential campaigns today are waged in no more than twenty states. That's great for Pennsylvania, Florida, Ohio, Wisconsin, Michigan, New Hampshire, and New Mexico, but not so great for Texas, New York, California, Massachusetts, Alabama, Oklahoma, Idaho, and Wyoming.

In fact, a popular vote system would force the candidates to run national campaigns because in a close election, you simply couldn't afford to neglect the votes in states like Delaware, Montana, the Dakotas, and Arizona.

It's time to make the Electoral College a thing of the past, just as we did with senators being elected by state legislatures!

While we are contemplating changes we need in our electoral process, we shouldn't forget that we should be doing everything we can to increase voter turnout (for example, Saturday voting, early voting, no requirement for absentee voting). Just as important, we should be doing all we can to beat back attempts to limit voting (like the craven effort by Republicans in many states to disenfranchise younger, minority, and older voters by requiring photo identification that many of them—who don't have cars and thereby don't have driver's licenses—can't produce).

3. Campaign Financing

As much as the first two changes are needed to improve our democracy, they pale in significance compared to our need to do something about the influence of money in politics. McCain-Feingold put real limits on the amount individuals and political action committees could give to federal candidates, including presidential candidates. It even limited the impact of the notorious 527s, the so-called issue advocacy groups, and, best of all, it required full disclosure of all contributions. It had some weaknesses: it still allowed givers to make significant donations to party committees such as the RNC or DNC and the Senate and House campaign committees, and it didn't eliminate the power of the 527s.

Nonetheless, it was a good start, but over the course of time the courts whittled away its effectiveness and then, in what has to be the worst and most outrageous decision since *Plessy v. Ferguson*, the US Supreme Court in the Citizens United case obliterated any attempts to reasonably control the influence of money in politics. It broke the time-honored federal limit on corporate giving and also opened the door to donations being made to impact elections without the necessity of disclosing them to the public.

Disclosure is absolutely essential in any fundraising plan. Although I believe limits and public financing are crucial to reduce the influence of special interests in our political system—while we are waiting for the constitutional changes that would allow limits to be put in place—full, complete, and on-time disclosure is crucial. At least if donations to candidates or super PACs must be disclosed well before the election, the public can judge whether a candidate has "sold out" to his contributors. In this year's Florida primary the Romney super PAC spent tens of millions of dollars carpet-bombing Newt Gingrich with effective negative ads. It was only after Floridians voted that it was disclosed that the super PAC had secured eight contributions from

Wall Street moguls of one million dollars or more. Would that knowledge have changed the votes of Florida Republicans? My guess is that it might have, but its effect would have been somewhat muted by the knowledge that casino magnate Sheldon Adelson had given Newt ten million dollars. It's just nuts.

Sometimes even disclosure requirements can be circumvented. In 1987, as I recounted, at the urging of the business community, I ran in the Democratic primary against incumbent mayor Wilson Goode. Businessmen who do business with the city are reluctant to contribute openly to a candidate running against an incumbent mayor for fear of retribution. One such businessman was a good friend who wanted me to win very badly, so every time I asked him for help he gave me a substantial check from a woman with a different last name. I asked him who she was, and he said it was his married sister who lived across the river in New Jersey. I checked, and she had significant net worth, so she could easily afford to make these contributions.

Well, I lost that race, but went on to run six more times, and she gave me large contributions in every race. Over a decade later I was attending a holiday party at the Union League in Philadelphia when a diminutive, attractive older lady came up to me and said, "You don't know me, but my name is Etta Winograd," and I said, "Yes I do, Etta. I have been looking at your name on checks and on my computer printouts of my major contributors for years!" We then shared a passionate hug. So much for full disclosure!

The story of Etta is humorous, but the Citizens United decision is no laughing matter. This turn of events is disastrous. It truly opens the floodgates. It insures that special interests—corporate interests mostly—will have an inordinate role in determining who wins or loses elections. But worse still, it means that these interests will thereby control and dominate federal legislation. The influence that special interests render in our political system is pernicious, and the main reason that our economic system has become patently unfair and the gap between the haves and the have-nots (a category that is growing far too swiftly) is growing wider and wider.

There is a solution, but because of the Supreme Court's decision, as I said, it will take a constitutional amendment to fix. The amendment must make it clear that political contributions are not "speech" and, therefore, can be limited or forbidden in some categories. This would allow for the reinstatement of the prohibition on corporate giving and an absolute requirement that all donations must be disclosed, and open the way for public financing of elections (which would help underfunded candidates compete in those five regional primaries).

The next step would be to bar any registered federal lobbyist from contributing to any federal candidate or committee. This type of law or rule could even pass constitutional muster now. For example, the Securities and Exchange Commission has adopted a regulation that no investment banker or underwriter who does business with a municipality or a state can contribute more that $250 to that state or municipal candidate. The rule was adopted, obviously, to prohibit people who work on governmental bond issues from enhancing their chances of being selected by a governmental official who received significant campaign contributions from that individual. In short, it banned influence-peddling, and a similar rule or law could do the same regarding the influence of lobbyists on federal legislation. Think of it—a lobbyist would have to persuade congressmen and senators by supplying them with facts and the rationale that supports what they want them to do as opposed to relying on the amount of campaign fundraising they have done to carry the day. Imagine having a process where lobbyists have a legitimate and appropriate role in trying to shape legislation by providing lawmakers with the facts and data they need to make a reasoned judgment.

So let's get busy. We can do this, guys. Let's pass the lobbyist law and begin the long, arduous process of amending the Constitution. It's hard, but it will *really* be worth it. (For information on the 28th Amendment drive, go to Dylan Rattigan's web site at http://www.dylanratigan.com/ and click on "Get Money Out.")

I know it's hard to amend the Constitution. I realize that the Equal Rights Amendment failed despite having millions of passionate women supporting it. But this change is vital to once again having a democracy "of the people, for the people, by the people." Let's not be defeatists, let's not wuss out. Let's work to take back our country. Memo to Occupiers: here's a cause you should adopt with fervor. It's a chance for you to actually change the influence of the one percenters rather than just bitch about it. We should all get off our cans and lead the charge. Don't be a bunch of whining wusses. The 28th Amendment could and should be the legacy of the Occupy movement!

Conclusion

The picture I have painted is one of our country at a crossroads, one heading in the wrong direction at an ever-increasing rate of speed. To use the entertainment vernacular, we've lost our mojo! Everyone talks about "American exceptionalism," and it has driven us for 236 years. I have talked about it previously, and it has set us apart from all other countries. It was our sense that we're different from everybody else. You didn't do it by inheritance here; you had to earn it by your own hard work, talent, and dedication. We all were free to dream of things that never were—as Robert Kennedy said so eloquently—and ask why not. And that freedom was encompassed in a pioneer spirit that convinced us that there was nothing we couldn't do, no challenge too tough for us, no hurdle too high for us to go over. That spirit led us to be, as I've said, the ultimate risk-takers, who invented new things, created bold projects, and innovated new idea after new idea.

That spirit, that sense of no limits appears to be gone, swallowed up by a fear of risk-taking. There don't appear to be too many candidates for a future *Profiles in Courage* to turn things around. Our problems mount, and there don't seem to be enough people willing to take on risk to begin the process of turning things around.

I had real hope that the super committee would decide that our economy was in such bad shape that they all needed to take a chance, compromise their rigid ideological positions, and create an agreement that reduced the deficit by $4 trillion or $5 trillion—far more than the $1.2 trillion they were charged to do. If they had done so, I believe it would have created an electricity in the American economy, which had expected the worst, and that would have spurred renewed confidence and renewed growth. When the committee basically gave up and started blaming one another, the thud could be heard around the world. Other nations were concluding that the United States simply was incapable of doing anything positive at all.

Sadly, it appears inevitable that nothing meaningful will get done during the rest of this election year—on jobs, infrastructure, or our exploding deficit. The consequences of this inaction are great. To the laid-off teacher or police officer, to the idle construction or factory worker, to the millions of other Americans who are desperately seeking work to help them to feed and care for their families, this delay until after the election is unconscionable. They all are at a loss to comprehend why our elected officials are so scared of doing anything that might anger anyone in this election year that Washington is totally paralyzed, a city run amok with wusses. And it isn't just the inaction, the failure to address our problems that's vexing, it is the pace of our delay. The revered Ronald Reagan said it best: "The bridges and highways we fail to repair today will have to be rebuilt tomorrow at many times the cost."

I believe there is a new D-day coming and that it will arrive early in 2013. Regardless of who wins the election, crucial decisions will have to be made. We are likely to have a divided government again, with both parties having some measure of control, but even if one party were to sweep the Presidency, Senate, and House, the filibuster rule in the Senate (requiring sixty votes to pass anything) mandates that there be a bipartisan approach once and for all to deal honestly and courageously with our problems. We will need to confront our deficit, and doing so means that both sides must show courage and take a political hit—the Democrats on entitlement cuts and the Republicans on raising revenues. We will need to begin to address our infrastructure needs and pass a robust, comprehensive six-year transportation bill to make us economically competitive again. We will need to stop importing everything and figure out a way to make things ourselves. We are going to have to find a way to once again invest in education, research, and innovation. We must create a plan for true energy independence for our nation, one that uses all of our natural resources wisely and well.

Can we do it, or have we become so wussified that we lack the will to take the risks necessary to create real solutions? I still believe that we can do it. There are individuals who have demonstrated real courage—a willingness to shoulder risks and make positive compromises: the senators and congressmen who voted to support the Simpson-Bowles Committee recommendations, which were great starting points for dealing with our deficit; Senator Jim Inhofe of Oklahoma, who, despite being one of the most conservative members of the Senate, understands and has voted for significantly increased investment in our infrastructure; Senator Tom Coburn, also of Oklahoma (Go Sooners!), who, despite being very conservative and a signatory to the no-tax pledge, had the guts to take on the new Wizard of Oz, Grover Norquist. When Grover said that ending the tax credit for ethanol would violate his antitax pledge and thus needed to be offset by tax cuts elsewhere, Senator Coburn pointed out that Grover was "defending wasteful spending." By the way, I believe that Grover is exactly like the Wizard of Oz—all bombastic bluster with no real reason to have power whatsoever, a true pretender.

On our side, I think that the work of Dick Durbin, John Kerry, and Chris Von Hollen in the super committee showed courage and a willingness to make things work. And last, the then one hundred members of the House who urged the super committee to do a big deal, including revenue and entitlement changes. These House members stated, "We write to you as a bipartisan group of representatives from across the political spectrum in the belief that the success of your committee is vital to our country's future. . . . Your committee has been given a unique opportunity and authority to act. We are prepared to support you in this effort."

We will need all of the above and more if we are to turn this country around. We also will need presidential leadership. My hope is that President Obama, if he is reelected, will be free from the burden of seeking office again (term-limited) and will be as consistently a bold and courageous risk-taker as he was in refusing to accept defeat on health care.

If we get that leadership from the top, if the risk-takers prevail in Congress, maybe we can say that American exceptionalism is back and we are wusses no more!

Well, I hope I've been able to convey to you the great experience I've had in my life in politics, and in doing so, made you laugh and think a little, too. It is my most fervent hope that I will continue to have the opportunity to influence the public dialogue. I hope that my work with NBC, MSNBC, and CNBC will let me do so, and I intend to keep up my work with Mayor Bloomberg for Building America's Future, advocating for a renewed and substantial commitment to revitalizing our nation's infrastructure.

As for running for office again, that simply isn't in my future. After having held three executive elected offices, I simply wouldn't be content as a legislator. When I make a decision, I want it to lead to immediate action. That happened often when I was DA, mayor, and governor. That would never happen as a senator. I would miss the action, and, besides, senators don't do much. In the great book *Prayer for the City*, Buzz Bissinger wrote about a train trip he and I took on our way back from Washington, DC. I had just testified before the Senate Finance Committee, with frustrating results. Buzz asked me if I would ever want to be a senator. I replied, "No. They don't do shit!" Buzz put this exchange in the book, but fortunately none of the senators read it, so it didn't hurt me during my time as governor, during which I had great success dealing with the US Senate. I guess I hope none of the senators read this book, either!

So I don't want to run for the Senate or any other legislative position, and the only executive office in politics that I haven't held is president, and no offense to the Granite or Hawkeye states, but I have no wish to spend two and half years of my life in New Hampshire and Iowa. But I do have one more race I want to run—not for me, but for Hillary Clinton. I would, for one last time, invest my heart and soul in trying to elect our first woman president.

Whatever happens in the future, I have loved the opportunity I have been given to serve. In the first forty-three years I have worked since graduating from law school, I have never made anything our society would call "real money," and I haven't missed it for a moment. Each day I have gotten up knowing that I'm using my talent and energy to make people's lives better. It's an incredible feeling that makes up for a lot. Would I do it over again? You bet!

ACKNOWLEDGMENTS

I would like to acknowledge and thank the following people who helped me in writing this book: David Cohen, Donna Cooper, Kaylan Dorsch, Alex Ficken, Jesse Rendell, and Kirstin Snow. I also want to thank countless members of my staff as DA, mayor, and governor who helped me remember many of the stories I relate here. The main reason I have been successful in public life is because of the great women and men who have tolerated my quirkiness and worked with me in the fight to improve the quality of life for the people of Philadelphia and Pennsylvania. Thank you all.

INDEX

McGarrigle, Tom, 165
McGovern, George, 212
McGrory, Mary, 91–92
McMichael, Morton, 170
McMichael Park, 170
McMutrie, Alison, 117–125
McMutrie, Jamie, 117–125
McNabb, Donovan, 130
media
  campaign fund-raising, 66–67
  gaming industry (Pennsylvania), 67–68
  Pennsylvania pay raise legislation, 65–66
  Philadelphia snow removal, 63–65
  politicians and, 210–211
Medicaid, 156
medical malpractice insurance, 194–196
Merrill, Herbie, 121, 122
Merrill, Leslie, 117–125
metallurgical coal, 177
minimum wage (2007), 105–106
mistakes, admitting, 210
Montgomery, Dave, 86
MOVE, 23–26, 30
Muhammad, Minister Rodney, 58

Napolitano, Janet, 207–208
National District Attorneys Association Conference, 14–15
National Governors' Association (2008), 154–155, 208

National Oceanic and Atmospheric Administration (NOAA), 138
National Rifle Association (NRA), 106–107
National Security Council, 120, 121
National Surface Transportation Policy and Revenue Study Commission, 175
Nation of Islam, 57–61
New Hampshire (2008), presidential primary, 144–145
New Yorker, 219
New York Post, 92
New York Times, 52, 59, 130, 166
NFL, 5–9
Nichol, Steve, 162–163
Nicholson, Jim, 95
Nixon, Richard, 212
Nobel Peace Prize, 167–168
Norman, Tony, 205
Norquist, Grover, 180–181, 193, 227
Norristown (Pennsylvania) High School, 108
Nutter, Michael, 132

Obama, Barack
  Affordable Care Act, 121, 124, 152, 157–158, 187, 191
  Economic Stimulus Act, 152–157, 178, 208
  future of, 228
  on Libya, 209–210